AN AMERICAN CULT: THE CORPORATION IS KILLING US

America has been sold a lie. The lie that corporations are the lifeblood of progress, the engines that drive our economy forward, and the pillars of our society. But here's the ugly truth: corporations aren't just companies—they've become cults. And just like any cult, they demand blind loyalty, obedience, and sacrifice. They consume everything in their path—our time, our labor, our dreams—and leave us with nothing but crumbs. This isn't just about profit. This is about control. A system where people's lives are ground into dust in service to the almighty bottom line.

DS

I appreciate you taking the time to think about this important topic.

Thank you.

-DS

Welcome to the Cult

America has been sold a lie. The lie that corporations are the lifeblood of progress, the engines that drive our economy forward, and the pillars of our society. But here's the ugly truth: corporations aren't just companies—they've become cults. And just like any cult, they demand blind loyalty, obedience, and sacrifice. They consume everything in their path—our time, our labor, our dreams—and leave us with nothing but crumbs. This isn't just about profit. This is about control. A system where people's lives are ground into dust in service to the almighty bottom line.

It's time we stopped pretending there's much difference between a corporate office and a cult compound. Just like cults, corporations have their own gods—profit and power—and their high priests, the CEOs and executives who demand unwavering faith. In exchange, they offer the illusion of safety, belonging, and purpose. You're promised that if you work hard enough, stay loyal enough, and give more than you've got, you'll be rewarded. But, in the end, you're left burned out and discarded.

The similarities are chilling: cults isolate their followers, break them down, and manipulate them into dependence. Corporations isolate their workers within rigid hierarchies, demanding more hours, more productivity, and more allegiance, all while cutting them off from any real sense of community or self-worth. Cults create a bubble of thought control—corporations have redefined the American workplace to the point where dissent is punished, and questioning the system is heresy.

But the rot goes deeper than just the workplace. Corporate power has infected every corner of American life. Our politics are bought, our education system is molded to produce obedient workers, and our media sings the praises of the very companies that exploit us. We're being brainwashed into believing this is how it has to be, that without these corporate overlords, society would collapse. In reality, it's the opposite: corporations are slowly but surely killing us, stripping away what's left of the American Dream and replacing it with a nightmare of endless work and vanishing rewards.

It's no coincidence that the middle class has been hollowed out, that wages have stagnated, that healthcare and education are out of reach for millions. This is by design. The corporate cult thrives on inequality and desperation, knowing that a frightened, struggling populace is easier to control. And as they tighten their grip on our lives, we continue to pledge our allegiance, thinking we have no other choice.

But it's time to wake up. The Corporation isn't just killing the American worker—it's killing the country. We are living in a system that benefits only a select few while leaving the rest of us to fend for scraps. It's a rigged game, a sick pyramid scheme where the ones at the top get richer and more powerful while the rest of us are left chasing after promises that will never be fulfilled.

This isn't capitalism; this is cultism. And it's time to break free.

From Dream to Machine

The Rise of the Corporate Cult

America once dreamed big. The promises of freedom, opportunity, and prosperity for all were woven into the fabric of the nation. Post-World War II, the American economy soared, driven by manufacturing, innovation, and a belief in the power of the worker. People believed in progress. There was a sense that hard work, skill, and ingenuity would be rewarded, and in many cases, it was. The American Dream—homeownership, a steady job, the ability to provide for one's family—felt attainable.

But what we didn't see coming was the quiet evolution of corporations from mere business entities into cultural, political, and economic forces that would dictate the terms of our lives. Corporations, once existing as mechanisms to create and distribute products, became something else entirely: they became machines of control.

By the late 20th century, corporations had transformed. No longer were they simply making things; they were making the rules. A corporation was no longer just a business entity producing goods and services. It became a system of power, shaping policy, culture, and ideology. The boardroom now held as much influence, if not more, than the halls of Congress.

What drove this shift? Greed, for one, but also a systematic effort to dismantle the institutions that once served as checks on corporate power. Labor unions, the bedrock of worker protection, were gutted through aggressive union-busting tactics and anti-labor legislation. Regulatory frameworks meant to ensure fair competition and protect consumers were systematically dismantled in the name of "free markets" and "efficiency." Slowly but surely, the corporation expanded its influence beyond the economy and into the core of American life.

The Hijacking of the American Dream

The idea of the American Dream was ripe for corporate exploitation. From the 1950s onward, corporations started selling a new version of the dream: one where success was defined by consumption and brand loyalty. They shifted the dream from one of hard work and reward to one where success was marked by the accumulation of things. Homes became bigger. Cars became more luxurious. Shopping became a pastime, a new way of defining personal identity.

But here's the catch: as we became more dependent on corporations to define our dreams, they simultaneously began to strip us of the very means to achieve them. Wages stagnated. Good, stable jobs that once provided security were outsourced or eliminated. The factory worker and middle manager were replaced by machines or lower-wage labor overseas. The corporations that had once built America were now dismantling it, brick by brick, job by job.

A key factor in this transformation was the ideological shift driven by economists and politicians who embraced neoliberalism—the belief that free markets, unfettered by government regulation, would lead to innovation and prosperity. This philosophy, embraced by Ronald Reagan and Margaret Thatcher in the 1980s, saw the dismantling of social safety nets, the deregulation of industries, and the lowering of corporate taxes. The result? Corporations were given free rein to maximize profits at any cost.

The American worker became expendable. Jobs that once provided stable incomes and benefits disappeared, outsourced to countries where labor was cheaper. The message from corporations was clear: loyalty to your job would no longer be rewarded. No matter how long you worked or how hard you toiled, you were always replaceable.

Meanwhile, corporations built a new kind of dream—the dream of endless growth. But growth for who? While CEOs and shareholders saw record profits, workers saw little to no benefit. The rise of stock buybacks, where companies would use their profits to buy their own stock to increase its value, instead of reinvesting in workers or infrastructure, exemplifies this perverse dynamic. The money flowed upward, leaving everyone else to fight for scraps.

The Shattering of the Social Contract

For much of the 20th century, there was an unspoken social contract between companies and workers. If you put in the effort, if you were loyal to your company, your company would take care of you. You'd have a job for life, decent pay, health benefits, and a pension to retire on. But starting in the late 20th century, corporations began systematically tearing apart this contract.

What was once a symbiotic relationship between companies and their employees morphed into something predatory. The new ethos of corporate America was about maximizing short-term profit at any cost, even if it meant gutting the very workforce that made that profit possible. Labor was redefined as an expense to be minimized rather than a resource to be cultivated.

In the 1990s, corporate downsizing became the new normal. Workers who had given decades of service were suddenly laid off en masse, replaced by cheaper labor or simply left unemployed. The drive to outsource jobs accelerated. Manufacturing, which had been the backbone of the American economy, was gutted as companies moved production to countries where labor laws were lax and wages were a fraction of what they were in the U.S.

Worse still, the corporate ideology began to seep into the public sector. Public services, once deemed sacrosanct, were privatized. Education, healthcare, prisons—these were no longer seen as social goods but as business opportunities. Corporations infiltrated every aspect of American life, ensuring that their bottom line trumped the public good.

And what did they give us in return? A shiny new cult of consumerism, where our value was no longer tied to our humanity or our contributions to society but to the brands we wore and the gadgets we bought. The once-proud working class was now a collection of wage slaves, forever chasing after the next paycheck, the next product, the next momentary hit of satisfaction.

Corporate Loyalty

It's important to understand that corporations have mastered the art of making their employees feel loyal to them without ever reciprocating that loyalty. Much like a cult leader who convinces his followers that they are part of something bigger, corporations sell the illusion of belonging and purpose. Employees are told they are part of a "family," that the corporation cares about them, values their contributions, and will reward their hard work.

In reality, nothing could be further from the truth. Employees are not family; they are expendable resources, to be used up and discarded when they are no longer needed. The moment a cheaper option becomes available—whether that's automation or outsourcing—the "family" is quick to show them the door.

Look at Amazon. The company refers to its warehouse workers as "associates" in a deliberate attempt to foster a sense of camaraderie and equality. But there's no equality when workers are forced to urinate in bottles to avoid missing quotas, or when injuries in warehouses are ignored to maintain productivity. Amazon's so-called associates are expendable. Loyalty is demanded, but it is never returned.

Growth at Any Cost

If there is a single guiding principle for corporations in modern America, it's this: growth. Growth at any cost, regardless of the toll it takes on workers, the environment, or society at large. Corporations are driven by an insatiable hunger for profit, and like any cult, they are never satisfied.

But who benefits from this growth? Not the workers. The gains of corporate growth are funneled upwards to a tiny elite—the CEOs and shareholders—while the vast majority of Americans see stagnant wages, rising costs, and dwindling job security. The pursuit of profit at any cost has led to environmental devastation, deepening inequality, and a fractured social fabric.

Corporations justify this relentless pursuit of growth by cloaking it in the language of progress. They argue that their success is society's success, that their innovations will lift all boats. But in reality, their success is built on the exploitation of their workers and the destruction of the planet. They feed us the same promises over and over again: that if we just work harder, buy more, and stay loyal, we will reap the rewards. But those rewards never come.

Corporations and Politics

As corporate power expanded in the economic realm, it wasn't long before these entities began to infiltrate another crucial aspect of American life—politics. Corporations didn't just grow more powerful by increasing their market share or expanding their operations; they began using their enormous wealth to influence the very mechanisms of democracy itself. Lobbying, campaign financing, and outright political manipulation became essential tools in the corporate arsenal.

Corporate America, it turns out, didn't just want to dominate the market; it wanted to write the rules. The rise of corporate lobbying in the late 20th and early 21st centuries has fundamentally undermined the democratic process. It created a system where politicians are more accountable to the executives who fund their campaigns than to the citizens who elect them.

Take, for example, the Citizens United decision in 2010, where the Supreme Court ruled that corporations, like individuals, have the right to spend unlimited amounts of money on political campaigns. This ruling marked the formalization of corporate control over American politics. Corporate money now flows into every corner of the political system, from presidential races to local elections. The result? A political system that serves corporate interests at the expense of the public.

The implications of this are staggering. Policies that could curb corporate excess—higher corporate taxes, stronger labor laws, environmental protections—are consistently blocked or watered down by politicians who are indebted to their corporate donors. The revolving door between corporate boardrooms and government offices ensures that the interests of the corporate elite remain prioritized over the needs of ordinary citizens. Former CEOs become government officials, and former government officials become corporate lobbyists, creating a closed loop of influence that's nearly impossible to break.

This isn't just an abstract problem. It directly affects the lives of millions of Americans. Consider healthcare, where corporate lobbyists from pharmaceutical and insurance companies ensure that meaningful reform remains off the table. The United States spends more on healthcare than any other nation, yet millions remain uninsured or burdened with crippling medical debt. Why? Because corporate interests have infiltrated the system so thoroughly that even basic measures, like reducing drug prices or expanding public healthcare options, are fiercely opposed by politicians on corporate payrolls.

Similarly, corporate influence over environmental policy has ensured that the U.S. remains a global laggard when it comes to addressing climate change. Fossil fuel companies spend millions to ensure that regulations are either nonexistent or toothless, while clean energy initiatives are buried under layers of bureaucratic red tape. Corporations that profit from the destruction of the environment use their political influence to ensure that nothing stands in the way of their bottom line—even if it means sacrificing the planet's future.

Dismantling Workers' Rights: The New Serfdom

Corporate infiltration into politics isn't just about preserving profits—it's about dismantling the rights of workers and ensuring they remain powerless. Since the 1970s, there has been a coordinated effort by corporations to destroy unions, undermine workers' rights, and dismantle the protections that once allowed the American middle class to thrive.

In the mid-20th century, nearly a third of all American workers were unionized. These unions fought for and won critical rights like fair wages, safe working conditions, and benefits. But today, union membership has plummeted to around 10%, with only 6% of private sector workers belonging to unions. This didn't happen by accident—it's the result of a calculated corporate assault on labor.

Corporations, with the help of compliant politicians, have engaged in aggressive union-busting efforts, using everything from legal maneuvers to intimidation to crush organized labor. In states across the country, "right-to-work" laws have been passed that weaken unions by allowing workers to benefit from union contracts without paying union dues. These laws, backed by corporate interests, have chipped away at workers' ability to organize and bargain collectively, leaving them at the mercy of their employers.

And what have corporations done with the power they've gained? They've replaced stable jobs with precarious, low-wage work. The rise of the gig economy—where workers are classified as independent contractors rather than employees—has allowed corporations to exploit millions of workers without offering them the benefits or protections of traditional employment. Companies like Uber, Lyft, and DoorDash have built billion-dollar empires on the backs of workers who are denied basic rights like healthcare, paid sick leave, and job security.

This is the new corporate serfdom: a system where workers are stripped of their rights, constantly underemployed, and left to fend for themselves in a precarious economic landscape. Corporations reap massive profits while workers are forced to hustle just to survive.

The Weaponization of Desperation

Perhaps the most insidious aspect of corporate control is how it exploits human desperation. When people are struggling to survive, when they're living paycheck to paycheck, they're far easier to control. Corporations know this, and they use it to their advantage. Whether it's by keeping wages low, denying healthcare, or exploiting the gig economy, corporations have learned that a desperate populace is a compliant populace.

Take the fast-food industry, which employs millions of low-wage workers. These corporations keep wages so low that many of their employees qualify for government assistance, effectively forcing taxpayers to subsidize corporate profits. Meanwhile, corporate executives take home millions in bonuses and stock options.

The same pattern is visible in industries like retail, where companies like Walmart dominate the market by paying workers poverty wages and denying them benefits. When workers do try to organize, they're met with aggressive union-busting tactics, intimidation, and firings. These companies thrive on desperation, knowing that as long as workers are desperate for a paycheck, they'll accept almost any condition, no matter how exploitative.

The Gig Economy: Freedom or Exploitation?

One of the most successful illusions corporations have sold is the idea that the gig economy represents freedom. Companies like Uber, Lyft, and Instacart have marketed themselves as liberators, offering workers the opportunity to "be their own boss" and work on their own terms. But in reality, the gig economy is just a more sophisticated form of exploitation.

Gig workers are denied the basic protections that come with traditional employment. They don't receive healthcare benefits, they don't have paid sick leave, and they're not guaranteed a minimum wage. Instead, they are treated as independent contractors, meaning they shoulder all the risk while the corporation reaps the rewards.

This model has proven immensely profitable for corporations. They've managed to offload the cost of employment onto the workers themselves, all while convincing the public that they're offering "opportunity." But for the vast majority of gig workers, the promise of freedom is a lie. They are trapped in a cycle of low pay, unpredictable hours, and constant hustle, with no real path to stability.

The Future of Corporate Domination

The trajectory we're on is clear: corporations will continue to consolidate power, widen inequality, and erode the rights of workers unless there is a fundamental shift in how we view and regulate them. Without drastic intervention, corporate domination will only intensify, leading to a future where the line between corporation and government becomes increasingly blurred.

Prominent political figures have already warned about the dangers of unchecked corporate power. In a 2023 interview, Senator Bernie Sanders commented on the growing influence of corporations, stating, "If we do not break up the enormous power of corporations and billionaires, we are headed toward a society where democracy is nothing more than a fig leaf covering corporate oligarchy. The stakes are clear: it's either them or us." (-Sanders, Bernie. *Interview with MSNBC: On Corporate Power and the Future of Democracy.* February 2023.)

The Hollowing Out of the Middle Class

The Death of Stable Employment

The American middle class, once the bedrock of the nation's economy and society, is now on life support. The promise of financial stability, homeownership, and a secure retirement—a cornerstone of the post-World War II American Dream—has been systematically dismantled. Over the past several decades, corporate America has waged an economic war on the middle class, stripping away decent wages, eliminating job security, and replacing stable employment with temporary gigs and precarious work. The result has been an unprecedented concentration of wealth in the hands of a few, while millions of Americans struggle to make ends meet.

One of the key drivers of middle-class decline has been the erosion of stable, well-paying jobs. In the post-war period, jobs were abundant, and many Americans could expect to work for a single company for most of their careers. They would start out in an entry-level position and, through hard work and loyalty, gradually rise up the ranks. Companies invested in their employees, offering competitive salaries, benefits, and pensions.

But by the late 20th century, this system was being dismantled. Corporations, obsessed with maximizing short-term profits, began slashing jobs, cutting benefits, and outsourcing work to countries with cheaper labor. The idea of a "job for life" quickly became a relic of the past. In its place, companies embraced a new model of temporary, contract, and part-time work that provided little to no security for employees.

Take the example of General Motors, once a symbol of American industrial strength. At its peak, GM employed hundreds of thousands of workers, offering well-paying jobs with excellent benefits. But as the company faced pressure from shareholders to cut costs and increase profits, it began slashing its workforce. By the early 21st century, GM had outsourced much of its manufacturing to Mexico and China, where labor was cheaper. The workers who remained in the U.S. were often forced to accept lower wages and reduced benefits. The effects were devastating for communities across the Midwest, where entire towns depended on GM plants for employment.

This story has been repeated across countless industries. Manufacturing jobs that once provided a pathway to the middle class have been replaced by low-wage service jobs, if they've been replaced at all. The steel industry, once a pillar of American manufacturing, has experienced a similar fate. In cities like Pittsburgh and Cleveland, steel mills that once employed tens of thousands of workers have been shuttered, leaving communities devastated by unemployment and poverty.

Wage Stagnation: Working Harder for Less

For those lucky enough to keep their jobs, the picture isn't much better. Over the past four decades, wages for most Americans have stagnated, while the cost of living has continued to rise. Between 1979 and 2019, productivity in the United States increased by 72%, but hourly wages grew by just 12% when adjusted for inflation. In other words, workers are producing more than ever, but they're seeing little of the reward.

This stagnation is not an accident. It's the result of deliberate corporate policies designed to keep wages low while funneling more and more profits to executives and shareholders. One of the most egregious examples of this is the use of stock buybacks. In the past, when companies made a profit, they would reinvest that money into their workforce—hiring more employees, raising wages, or improving benefits. But in recent decades, companies have increasingly used profits to buy back their own stock, driving up share prices and enriching executives whose compensation is often tied to the value of the company's stock.

Consider Walmart, the largest employer in the United States. Despite earning billions in profits each year, Walmart has been notoriously stingy when it comes to paying its employees. Most Walmart workers earn wages so low that they qualify for government assistance, including food stamps and Medicaid. In 2018, Walmart announced a $20 billion stock buyback program, enriching shareholders and executives while leaving its workers to rely on public assistance to survive. This is not an isolated incident; it's the modus operandi of corporate America.

The wage stagnation crisis extends beyond retail. Across industries, companies have adopted policies that keep wages low while maximizing executive compensation. In the tech industry, for example, companies like Amazon and Apple rake in billions in profits while paying many of their workers—particularly those in warehouses or retail—barely enough to live on. The gap between worker productivity and wages has become a chasm, and that gap is filled by the growing wealth of the corporate elite.

The Gig Economy: Freedom or Exploitation?

At the same time that traditional jobs were being destroyed, a new form of work was being born: the gig economy. Companies like Uber, Lyft, and DoorDash promised workers freedom and flexibility, allowing them to set their own hours and be their own bosses. But the reality of gig work is far less glamorous. Gig workers are classified as independent contractors, meaning they are not entitled to the same protections as employees. They don't receive health insurance, they aren't guaranteed a minimum wage, and they have no job security.

For many gig workers, this so-called "freedom" means working longer hours for less pay, with none of the benefits that come with traditional employment. Uber drivers, for instance, are often forced to work 60 to 80 hours a week just to cover their expenses, and their pay can fluctuate wildly depending on demand and the company's ever-changing algorithms. Many drivers have reported making less than minimum wage once expenses like gas, insurance, and vehicle maintenance are factored in.

The gig economy also reflects the broader trend of corporations shifting the costs and risks of employment onto workers themselves. Instead of investing in their workforce, companies like Uber and Lyft have found a way to extract labor without providing any of the protections or benefits that are standard in traditional employment. And while gig workers may be classified as independent contractors, they are anything but independent. They are subject to the whims of corporate algorithms, forced to compete for work in an oversaturated market where supply far exceeds demand.

The consequences of this shift are profound. The gig economy has created a new class of precarious workers who have little to no financial security. Without health insurance or retirement benefits, gig workers are left to navigate an increasingly expensive and unstable economy on their own. This economic instability has ripple effects throughout society, contributing to the rise of household debt, increased reliance on government assistance, and growing inequality.

The Disappearance of Benefits and Pensions

Another key pillar of middle-class stability—benefits and pensions—has been systematically dismantled by corporate America. In the mid-20th century, many companies offered generous benefits packages that included health insurance, paid vacation, and pensions. These benefits provided workers with a safety net, ensuring that they could access healthcare and retire with dignity.

But over the past several decades, companies have shifted away from providing these benefits, opting instead for cost-cutting measures that leave workers exposed to financial hardship. One of the most significant changes has been the decline of employer-sponsored pensions. In 1980, 60% of private-sector workers had access to a defined-benefit pension plan, which guaranteed them a fixed income in retirement. By 2020, that number had fallen to just 15%.

Instead of pensions, companies now offer 401(k) plans, which shift the responsibility of saving for retirement onto workers themselves. While 401(k) plans can be a useful savings tool, they are far less secure than traditional pensions. Workers must manage their own investments, and their retirement savings are subject to the whims of the stock market. For many workers, particularly those in low-wage jobs, it is nearly impossible to save enough for a secure retirement through a 401(k) plan.

Health insurance, too, has become increasingly unaffordable for workers. Companies that once provided comprehensive health benefits have shifted more of the cost onto employees, forcing them to pay higher premiums, deductibles, and co-pays. As a result, many workers now have health insurance that is technically available but practically out of reach due to the high cost of care.

One of the most glaring examples of this shift is the rise of part-time and contract work. By classifying workers as part-time or contract employees, companies can avoid offering benefits altogether. This practice is rampant in industries like retail, where companies like Amazon and Walmart employ hundreds of thousands of part-time workers who are not eligible for benefits, despite working full-time hours. These workers are left to navigate the expensive and complex healthcare system on their own, often forgoing necessary care due to the cost.

Corporate Tax Cuts and Shifting the Burden to the Middle Class

While corporations have been slashing wages, eliminating benefits, and outsourcing jobs, they've also been receiving massive tax breaks from the federal government. Corporate America has lobbied aggressively for lower taxes, and politicians have been all too willing to comply. The result is a tax system that overwhelmingly benefits the wealthy and leaves the middle class to pick up the tab.

The 2017 Tax Cuts and Jobs Act, passed under the Trump administration, is a prime example of this dynamic. The law slashed the corporate tax rate from 35% to 21%, delivering a windfall to the largest corporations and their shareholders. While the tax cuts were sold as a way to spur economic growth and benefit workers, the reality is that most of the gains went to corporate executives and wealthy investors. Corporations used the money to buy back their own stock, driving up share prices and enriching those at the top, while wages for workers remained stagnant.

At the same time, the tax burden has increasingly shifted to the middle class. As corporate taxes have fallen, governments at the state and local levels have raised taxes on ordinary citizens to make up the shortfall. Sales taxes, property taxes, and other regressive forms of taxation disproportionately affect middle- and low-income Americans, exacerbating economic inequality.

An Economy Rigged Against the Middle Class

The economic devastation wrought by corporate America has hollowed out the middle class and created a society where wealth is concentrated in the hands of a few, while the rest of the population struggles to survive. Stable jobs have been replaced by precarious gig work, wages have stagnated, and benefits have been stripped away. Meanwhile, corporations continue to rake in record profits, enriched by stock buybacks and tax cuts, while the middle class is left to bear the brunt of economic hardship.

The system is rigged, and unless there is a fundamental shift in how we structure our economy, the American middle class will continue to erode. The once-great engine of the American Dream has been dismantled piece by piece, leaving behind a hollow shell of what it once was. And as corporations continue to wield unchecked power, the future looks bleak for those hoping to reclaim even a fraction of the stability and opportunity that the middle class once enjoyed.

A New Form of Exploitation

The gig economy was sold as the future of work, a new paradigm where workers could enjoy freedom, flexibility, and independence. No longer tethered to the traditional nine-to-five grind, gig workers were promised the ability to set their own hours, be their own bosses, and choose the jobs they wanted. Companies like Uber, Lyft, DoorDash, and Instacart painted an enticing picture of a world where work fit seamlessly into people's lives, allowing them to earn money on their terms.

But the reality of the gig economy is far darker than its shiny marketing campaigns suggest. Beneath the surface of this so-called revolution lies a system built on exploitation, where workers bear the brunt of economic risk while corporations reap the rewards. For the millions of gig workers who rely on these platforms to make a living, the promised freedom has been nothing more than an illusion. Instead, they find themselves trapped in a cycle of low pay, unpredictable hours, and little to no legal protections. The gig economy has become a modern-day form of exploitation, where corporations have found new ways to profit off labor while shirking responsibility for workers' rights.

At the heart of the gig economy's exploitative nature is the classification of workers as "independent contractors" rather than employees. This distinction allows companies to sidestep labor laws that were designed to protect workers. Independent contractors are not entitled to minimum wage protections, overtime pay, health benefits, or paid sick leave. They also aren't eligible for unemployment benefits or workers' compensation, leaving them vulnerable if they are injured on the job or if demand for their services suddenly dries up.

Gig companies argue that this classification benefits workers by offering them flexibility. But for most gig workers, the flexibility is a mirage. To make a living wage, many workers must put in long, grueling hours with no guarantee of steady income. And because they are classified as independent contractors, they must cover all their own expenses—fuel, car maintenance, insurance, and even phone data plans to access the platforms they work for. Once these expenses are factored in, many gig workers find that their real earnings are far below minimum wage.

One of the most prominent examples of this exploitation is Uber, the ride-hailing giant that has become synonymous with the gig economy. Uber markets itself as a platform that empowers drivers to be their own bosses, but the reality is far different. Uber's drivers are subject to the whims of the company's algorithm, which dictates when and where they can work, how much they will be paid, and even whether they will continue to have access to the platform. Drivers are given little transparency into how Uber's algorithm calculates pay, and the company frequently changes its payment structure without warning or input from drivers. This leaves many drivers struggling to make a living wage despite working full-time or even more.

The Uber and Lyft Fight: California's Prop 22

One of the most prominent cases of gig workers being exploited occurred in California in 2020, during the fight over

Proposition 22, a ballot measure backed by Uber, Lyft, and other gig economy giants. The fight over Prop 22 illustrates just how far gig companies will go to protect their profits at the expense of workers' rights.

In 2019, California passed **Assembly Bill 5 (AB5)**, a landmark piece of legislation that sought to reclassify gig workers as employees, rather than independent contractors. This law would have entitled gig workers to a host of benefits that traditional employees enjoy, including minimum wage protections, health benefits, and the right to unionize. For gig workers who had been toiling for years with little to no security, AB5 represented a potential breakthrough in the fight for fair treatment.

But Uber, Lyft, DoorDash, and other gig companies had no intention of letting this law stand. They immediately launched a massive, multi-million-dollar lobbying effort to exempt themselves from AB5, arguing that it would destroy the flexibility that gig workers supposedly valued. When that effort failed, the companies took their fight to the ballot box, sponsoring Prop 22 to overturn the core provisions of AB5.

The gig companies poured over $200 million into the Prop 22 campaign, making it the most expensive ballot measure in California's history. They flooded the airwaves with advertisements claiming that reclassifying gig workers as employees would force them to cut jobs, raise prices, and eliminate the flexibility that workers cherished. The companies even went as far as to insert pro-Prop 22 messages directly into their apps, pressuring drivers and customers alike to support the measure.

Despite opposition from labor groups and worker advocates, Prop 22 passed in November 2020, with 59% of the vote. The passage of Prop 22 was a devastating blow to gig workers. It codified their status as independent contractors, exempting gig companies from many of the labor laws that protect traditional workers. While the measure did offer some limited benefits, such as a health insurance stipend for drivers who work more than 15 hours a week, it fell far short of providing the comprehensive protections that employee status would have guaranteed.

The aftermath of Prop 22 has been brutal for gig workers. A 2021 study by the **UC Berkeley Labor Center** found that after accounting for expenses like gas, maintenance, and insurance, most Uber and Lyft drivers were earning less than California's minimum wage, despite the claims made by the gig companies during the Prop 22 campaign. The study also found that the health insurance stipend offered under Prop 22 only covered a small fraction of drivers, and the vast majority of workers were left without access to affordable healthcare.

The passage of Prop 22 set a dangerous precedent, signaling to corporations that they could buy their way out of labor laws through massive spending on political campaigns. It also demonstrated the lengths to which gig companies would go to protect their business model, even if it meant leaving their workers without basic protections. The case of Prop 22 shows that in the gig economy, profits come first, and workers' rights come last.

Algorithmic Control

One of the most insidious aspects of the gig economy is the way that workers are controlled by algorithms rather than human managers. Gig companies like Uber and DoorDash have perfected the art of algorithmic management, using complex, opaque algorithms to dictate nearly every aspect of a worker's experience on the platform. These algorithms determine when and where work is available, how much workers will be paid, and how they will be evaluated.

For many gig workers, the algorithm is an invisible boss, constantly monitoring their performance and dictating their behavior. Uber drivers, for instance, are subject to a rating system where passengers rate their experience on a scale of one to five stars. Drivers who fall below a certain rating threshold risk being deactivated from the platform, effectively losing their jobs. But the rating system is often arbitrary and unfair—drivers can receive low ratings for things beyond their control, such as traffic delays or passengers' mood. And because Uber refuses to provide detailed feedback on why a driver's rating has dropped, drivers are left in a constant state of anxiety, unsure of how to improve or avoid deactivation.

In addition to ratings, gig workers are subjected to dynamic pricing algorithms that can change their pay at a moment's notice. Uber's surge pricing system, for example, raises fares during times of high demand, but the company takes a large cut of the increased fare, leaving drivers with only a small portion of the extra money. Drivers have no control over when surge pricing is activated or how much they will earn from it, creating a sense of unpredictability that makes it difficult to plan their finances.

Algorithmic control strips gig workers of autonomy while giving corporations plausible deniability for their exploitative practices. When workers are mistreated, companies can simply point to the algorithm and claim that the system is objective and fair. But in reality, the algorithms are designed to maximize corporate profits, often at the expense of workers' livelihoods.

The Illusion of Flexibility

One of the central selling points of the gig economy is the idea of flexibility—the promise that workers can choose when, where, and how much they want to work. But for many gig workers, this flexibility is an illusion. While workers may technically be able to log on and off the platform at will, the reality is that they are often forced to work long, unpredictable hours to make ends meet.

For Uber drivers, the flexibility to choose when to work is limited by the company's demand algorithms, which dictate when rides are available and how much drivers will be paid. During peak hours, when demand is high, drivers may earn a decent wage, but during off-peak hours, earnings can be so low that it's not worth driving at all. Many drivers report being forced to work long hours, often during evenings and weekends, just to scrape together enough money to cover their expenses.

For delivery drivers working for platforms like DoorDash and Instacart, the situation is much the same. Workers are subject to ever-changing pay structures and unpredictable demand, making it difficult to plan their work schedules. Some drivers report accepting multiple deliveries at once just to make a livable wage, but this comes with its own set of challenges—long wait times at restaurants, multiple stops on a single trip, and the constant pressure to deliver quickly to avoid negative ratings.

The flexibility that gig companies advertise is ultimately a mirage, designed to lure workers into a system that offers little stability or security. For most gig workers, the reality is one of long hours, low pay, and constant uncertainty.

Legal Battles and Worker Pushback

Despite the overwhelming power of gig companies, workers have begun to fight back. In recent years, gig workers across the country have organized protests, strikes, and legal challenges in an effort to secure better pay and working conditions. One of the most high-profile legal battles took place in New York City, where Uber and Lyft drivers successfully fought for a minimum wage law that ensures they are paid at least $17.22 per hour after expenses. This victory represented a significant step forward in the fight for gig workers' rights, but it was hard-won, and similar efforts have faced fierce opposition in other states.

In addition to legal battles, gig workers have taken their fight to the streets. In 2019, drivers in cities across the U.S. staged strikes in protest of low pay and poor working conditions, demanding higher wages, better transparency, and the right to unionize. These protests garnered national attention, shining a spotlight on the exploitation that underpins the gig economy.

While these efforts have achieved some success, the gig companies' vast resources and political influence make it difficult for workers to secure lasting change. As the fight for gig workers' rights continues, it is clear that the gig economy represents a new frontier in the struggle between labor and capital, where workers must constantly push back against the exploitation that lies at the heart of the business model.

A System Built on Exploitation

The gig economy, far from being the future of work, is a modern-day form of exploitation. Gig workers are denied basic labor protections, subject to the whims of corporate algorithms, and forced to bear the costs and risks of employment on their own. The fight over Prop 22 in California was a stark reminder of the power imbalance between gig companies and their workers, and it set a dangerous precedent for the future of labor in America.

As long as corporations are allowed to classify their workers as independent contractors, they will continue to exploit this loophole to maximize their profits at the expense of workers' rights. The gig economy is not a system that empowers workers; it is a system that enriches corporations while leaving workers vulnerable and disposable. And unless there is a fundamental shift in the way we regulate these companies, millions of gig workers will remain trapped in this cycle of exploitation.

The Rise of Precarious Work and Financial Instability

The American economy is built on a foundation of economic inequality, and nowhere is this more evident than in the way corporations have weaponized economic despair to maintain control over workers and entrench their power. Over the past several decades, corporations have perfected the art of exploiting economic insecurity, ensuring that millions of Americans are trapped in a perpetual state of anxiety about their financial futures. This insecurity, coupled with the deliberate dismantling of labor protections and the rise of predatory financial practices, has created a system in which workers are too desperate and vulnerable to challenge the status quo.

Economic despair is not an unfortunate byproduct of corporate greed—it is a deliberate strategy. By keeping wages low, benefits scarce, and job security nonexistent, corporations have created a labor force that is too fearful of losing what little they have to demand more. As a result, the American worker is constantly walking a financial tightrope, struggling to make ends meet while corporate profits soar to record levels.

One of the primary ways corporations have weaponized economic despair is through the rise of precarious, low-wage work. In the decades following World War II, stable, full-time employment with decent wages and benefits was the norm for much of the American workforce. This stability allowed millions of Americans to achieve financial security, buy homes, raise families, and retire with dignity.

But starting in the late 20th century, corporations began to dismantle this system of stable employment. Full-time jobs with benefits were replaced with part-time, temporary, and contract work. As we've seen with the rise of the gig economy, corporations have increasingly shifted the burden of financial risk onto workers themselves, leaving them without the safety nets that once allowed them to thrive.

Precarious work has become the norm in industries ranging from retail and hospitality to healthcare and education. Workers in these industries often have little control over their schedules, receive few or no benefits, and are paid wages so low that they struggle to meet their basic needs. The rise of part-time work is particularly troubling, as it allows companies to avoid providing health insurance and other benefits that are typically reserved for full-time employees. Workers are left scrambling to piece together enough hours to survive, often working multiple jobs just to cover rent and groceries.

Walmart, the largest private employer in the United States, is a prime example of this practice. The company has long been criticized for its reliance on part-time workers who are paid low wages and denied access to benefits like health insurance. In 2019, a report from the **UC Berkeley Labor Center** found that nearly half of Walmart's employees relied on public assistance programs like food stamps and Medicaid to make ends meet, despite working for one of the most profitable companies in the world. This isn't an isolated case; it is emblematic of a broader trend where corporations rely on low wages and precarious employment while shifting the cost of social support onto the government.

The result of this shift has been an explosion of economic insecurity. Millions of workers live paycheck to paycheck, one unexpected expense away from financial ruin. A 2019 survey by the **Federal Reserve** found that nearly 40% of Americans would struggle to come up with $400 in an emergency. This level of financial instability leaves workers with little bargaining power and makes them vulnerable to exploitation. When workers are desperate to keep their jobs, they are far less likely to demand higher wages, better working conditions, or union representation.

The Trap of Debt or Modern-Day Serfdom

Another key aspect of how corporations have weaponized economic despair is through the use of debt as a tool of control. In the absence of a living wage, affordable healthcare, and accessible education, many Americans have been forced to turn to credit to cover their basic needs. As wages have stagnated and costs have risen, debt has become a defining feature of the American experience, particularly for the working class.

The explosion of household debt in America is staggering. In 2020, total household debt reached a record $14.35 trillion, with mortgage, student loan, credit card, and auto loan debt all contributing to the burden. For many Americans, debt has become a form of modern-day serfdom, chaining them to their jobs and limiting their ability to seek better opportunities or challenge their employers. The fear of missing a mortgage payment or defaulting on a student loan keeps workers tethered to jobs they might otherwise leave, even when those jobs are exploitative.

Student loan debt, in particular, has become a crushing burden for millions of Americans. As the cost of higher education has skyrocketed, students have been forced to take on ever-larger loans to pay for their education. The result is a generation of workers saddled with massive amounts of debt, with little prospect of paying it off. In 2021, the total amount of student loan debt in the United States exceeded $1.7 trillion, and many borrowers face decades of repayment, often without seeing a significant improvement in their financial situation. The student loan crisis disproportionately affects low-income and minority borrowers, deepening existing inequalities.

For corporations, this debt represents an opportunity. Workers who are drowning in debt are far less likely to take risks, such as quitting a low-paying job to pursue better opportunities or joining a union to demand fair treatment. Instead, they are more likely to accept the terms set by their employers, no matter how exploitative, out of fear of losing their income and defaulting on their loans. In this way, debt becomes a tool of control, keeping workers compliant and fearful of challenging the corporate status quo.

The Healthcare Trap

The United States' uniquely expensive and inaccessible healthcare system is another weapon corporations use to trap workers in cycles of economic despair. Unlike many developed countries, where healthcare is considered a basic right, healthcare in the U.S. is largely tied to employment. This means that for many workers, losing their job also means losing access to affordable healthcare. This dynamic is a powerful tool of control, forcing workers to remain in jobs they might otherwise leave for fear of losing their health coverage.

For low-wage workers, access to healthcare is often precarious at best. Many part-time, gig, and contract workers are not offered employer-sponsored health insurance, and even when it is available, the cost of premiums and deductibles can be prohibitively expensive. As a result, many workers are forced to go without health coverage or rely on inadequate plans that leave them vulnerable to medical debt.

Medical debt is a particularly insidious form of financial despair. A 2021 report from the **Consumer Financial Protection Bureau (CFPB)** found that medical debt was the most common type of debt in collections, affecting more than 20% of U.S. households. Even for those with insurance, the high cost of deductibles and co-pays can lead to financial hardship. For many workers, the fear of incurring medical debt is a powerful deterrent to leaving a job, even if that job is underpaid or exploitative.

The healthcare trap is especially evident in industries like retail and food service, where low-wage workers are often denied access to health benefits. In these industries, the fear of losing healthcare coverage forces workers to accept low wages, unpredictable hours, and unsafe working conditions. This dynamic is compounded by the fact that many of these workers are in physically demanding jobs that put them at risk of injury. Without adequate health coverage, an injury can lead to financial ruin, further entrenching workers in cycles of economic despair.

The Psychological Toll of Economic Despair

While the financial consequences of economic insecurity are devastating, the psychological toll can be just as harmful. Living in a state of constant financial anxiety can have profound effects on mental health, leading to increased rates of stress, depression, and even physical illness. For many workers, the daily struggle to make ends meet takes a heavy emotional toll, sapping their energy and leaving them feeling hopeless about their futures.

Research has shown that economic insecurity is closely linked to mental health problems. A 2019 study by the **American Psychological Association** found that financial stress was one of the most common sources of stress for Americans, with nearly 60% of respondents reporting that money was a significant source of stress in their lives. The constant pressure to pay bills, keep up with rising living costs, and avoid falling into debt can lead to chronic stress, which in turn can contribute to a host of physical and mental health problems, including anxiety, depression, and heart disease.

For workers who are already struggling to make ends meet, the added stress of precarious employment and low wages can be overwhelming. The fear of losing a job, falling into debt, or being unable to afford medical care creates a sense of powerlessness that can have lasting psychological effects. In many cases, workers who are trapped in cycles of economic despair feel as though they have no control over their lives, leading to feelings of hopelessness and despair.

This psychological toll has broader societal implications as well. When large segments of the population are living in a state of financial and emotional distress, it undermines social cohesion and contributes to a sense of collective despair. The rise of opioid addiction, suicide, and mental health crises in the United States can be directly linked to the economic conditions that have left millions of Americans feeling trapped and abandoned by a system that prioritizes corporate profits over human well-being.

A System Designed to Exploit

The weaponization of economic despair is one of the most insidious tactics used by corporate America to maintain control over the workforce. By creating a system where workers are constantly teetering on the edge of financial ruin, corporations have ensured that their employees remain too desperate and fearful to demand fair wages, benefits, or working conditions. Whether through the rise of precarious work, the burden of debt, the healthcare trap, or the psychological toll of economic insecurity, corporations have mastered the art of keeping workers in a state of perpetual vulnerability.

This system is not accidental—it is by design. Corporations have deliberately dismantled the safety nets that once protected workers, replacing stable jobs with precarious ones, shifting the burden of healthcare and retirement onto individuals, and using debt as a tool of control. The result is a workforce that is too economically insecure to challenge the corporate stranglehold on their lives.

As long as corporations are allowed to wield economic despair as a weapon, the American middle class will continue to erode, and the gap between the wealthy and the rest of the population will continue to widen. The only way to break this cycle is through collective action—by rebuilding the labor movement, demanding comprehensive healthcare reform, and fighting for policies that prioritize the well-being of workers over corporate profits.

The Cult of Productivity

The Rise of Hustle Culture

In today's corporate-driven America, there's a new kind of religion, and it doesn't worship gods or saints—it worships work. The cult of productivity has infiltrated every corner of American life, dictating not just how people work, but how they view their own value and purpose. This obsession with productivity has been meticulously cultivated by corporations, where endless work is glorified and burnout is worn as a badge of honor. As a result, the lines between personal life and professional identity have been erased, leaving workers mentally and physically exhausted while corporations reap the rewards.

This worship of work isn't just an unhealthy cultural trend—it's a deliberate and systemic manipulation. By convincing workers that their worth is tied to how much they produce, corporations have engineered a society where people willingly sacrifice their time, health, and relationships for the promise of success that, for most, never materializes. The result is a workforce that is constantly overworked, underpaid, and trapped in a cycle of endless hustle.

The rise of hustle culture—the belief that constant work and striving are necessary to achieve success—didn't happen by accident. It was the product of a deliberate corporate strategy to instill a sense of duty, loyalty, and ambition in workers. Hustle culture tells us that we should always be grinding, always be improving, and always be hustling for more. Rest is seen as weakness, and taking time off is considered lazy or uncommitted.

For many workers, the ideal of hustle culture is epitomized by Silicon Valley, where tech entrepreneurs like Elon Musk and Mark Zuckerberg have cultivated an image of tireless work ethic and nonstop innovation. Musk famously once said, "Nobody ever changed the world on 40 hours a week." This mindset has seeped into workplaces across the country, where employees are expected to work long hours, often without extra pay, in pursuit of an elusive dream of advancement and success.

But this fetishization of work is a lie. While the promise of upward mobility is constantly dangled in front of workers, the reality is that very few will actually reap the benefits. The vast majority of employees are simply working harder and longer, with little to show for it beyond exhaustion and frustration. In many cases, the pursuit of productivity has become an endless treadmill, where no matter how fast workers run, they never seem to get ahead.

The Exploitation of Ambition

Corporations have become masters at exploiting workers' ambition, convincing them that their personal success is tied directly to the company's success. The corporate messaging is subtle but pervasive: if you work hard enough, if you're dedicated enough, you will be rewarded. Promotions, raises, recognition—they are all within your grasp, but only if you push yourself beyond your limits.

In reality, this is a classic bait-and-switch. While a few workers may rise through the ranks, most find themselves stuck in dead-end jobs with no real path to advancement. The promise of future success is used as a tool to extract more labor from employees, who believe that their sacrifices will eventually pay off. Corporations create this illusion of meritocracy, but the deck is stacked against most workers from the start.

One of the most glaring examples of this exploitation is found in the tech industry, where employees are often lured by the promise of stock options and potential IPO windfalls. Companies like Uber, Airbnb, and WeWork have built entire workforces based on the idea that employees should put in grueling hours and sacrifice their personal lives for the greater good of the company—because one day, when the company goes public, they'll be rich.

But for most employees, that day never comes. Instead, they find themselves working 60- to 80-hour weeks with little more than empty promises and stock options that never materialize into anything meaningful. Meanwhile, the executives and early investors cash out, leaving workers with nothing but the toll that years of overwork have taken on their mental and physical health.

The Manipulation of Identity and Self-Worth

One of the most insidious aspects of the cult of productivity is the way it has warped how people view their own self-worth. In corporate America, workers are encouraged to define themselves not by their relationships, hobbies, or personal fulfillment, but by their job titles and output. Productivity becomes the metric by which people are judged—not just by their employers, but by society at large and even by themselves.

This manipulation of identity is a deliberate corporate strategy. By encouraging workers to tie their sense of worth to their productivity, corporations can ensure that employees will continue to work harder and longer, even at the expense of their own well-being. If you believe that your value as a person is directly linked to how much you produce, then you are far less likely to push back against overwork, demand higher wages, or take time off.

The damage that this mentality does to workers is profound. When people are constantly told that they aren't doing enough, that they aren't productive enough, they begin to internalize these messages. Burnout, anxiety, and depression become common, but rather than recognizing these as signs of a toxic system, workers are often made to feel that their struggles are a personal failing. If you're tired, stressed, or overwhelmed, it's not because the system is broken—it's because you're not working hard enough.

This dynamic is particularly damaging in industries where creativity and innovation are prized. In these fields, workers are often told that they must constantly be creating, producing, and coming up with new ideas. But creativity doesn't thrive in an environment of constant pressure and exhaustion. The more workers are pushed to produce, the less they are able to innovate, leading to a cycle where burnout stifles the very creativity that companies claim to value.

Overwork as a Badge of Honor

In the cult of productivity, overwork is celebrated. The longer hours you put in, the more dedicated you are. In many workplaces, employees boast about how little sleep they've gotten, how many hours they've spent at the office, or how long it's been since they took a vacation. These behaviors are seen not as signs of imbalance, but as indicators of success.

This culture of overwork is particularly toxic in industries like finance, law, and tech, where long hours are not only expected but required to succeed. In these fields, the workday doesn't end when you leave the office—employees are expected to be available around the clock, responding to emails and phone calls at all hours. The result is a workforce that is always "on," with no separation between work and personal life.

In 2019, a report by the **World Health Organization (WHO)** revealed that overwork was responsible for the deaths of hundreds of thousands of people each year, with long working hours significantly increasing the risk of stroke and heart disease. Despite the mounting evidence that overwork is literally killing people, the corporate world continues to celebrate it as a sign of dedication and commitment.

The normalization of overwork is not just unhealthy—it's exploitative. By encouraging workers to glorify overwork, corporations are able to extract more labor from their employees without offering any additional compensation. Workers are made to feel guilty for taking time off, and vacations are often seen as a luxury that only the lazy or unmotivated indulge in.

The Dismantling of Work-Life Boundaries

One of the most damaging effects of the cult of productivity is the erosion of boundaries between work and personal life. With the rise of remote work, constant connectivity, and the expectation of 24/7 availability, the traditional separation between the office and home has all but disappeared. For many workers, this has created a situation where they are never truly off the clock.

The COVID-19 pandemic accelerated this trend, as millions of workers shifted to remote work and found themselves navigating a new world where the lines between work and home life blurred beyond recognition. While working from home offers some benefits, it has also led to an environment where workers are expected to be available at all times, with emails and Zoom meetings creeping into what was once personal time.

Corporations have embraced this shift, framing it as a sign of progress and flexibility. But in reality, the dissolution of work-life boundaries has only further entrenched the cult of productivity. Workers are now expected to be available for longer hours, with fewer breaks, and with even more demands placed on their time. The idea of a true "day off" has become a thing of the past, replaced by the constant expectation of availability and responsiveness.

The consequences of this are profound. Workers are finding it increasingly difficult to maintain a healthy work-life balance, leading to higher rates of burnout, stress, and mental health issues. But despite the clear evidence that overwork is damaging, corporations continue to push the idea that productivity is the ultimate measure of success, leaving workers trapped in a cycle of endless labor.

The Cult of Productivity and Corporate Control

The cult of productivity isn't just a cultural phenomenon—it's a tool of corporate control. By convincing workers that their worth is tied to their output, corporations have created a system where employees willingly sacrifice their health, well-being, and personal lives in pursuit of an unattainable ideal. This obsession with productivity has eroded the boundaries between work and personal life, leaving workers overworked, underpaid, and constantly exhausted.

The glorification of overwork serves only one purpose: to extract more labor from workers without compensating them fairly. And as long as workers continue to buy into the myth that their value is determined by how much they produce, corporations will continue to exploit them. The cult of productivity is not just harmful—it's a deliberate strategy to maintain corporate control and keep workers in a state of perpetual hustle.

The Corporate Sacrifice

It's time to get real: burnout is not some unfortunate side effect of modern work—it's the business model. Corporate America thrives on it, exploits it, and then has the audacity to act like it's some personal failing when workers finally collapse under the pressure. This isn't about productivity, efficiency, or even economic growth; it's about extracting every last ounce of energy from workers before discarding them and moving on to the next. The system isn't broken—this is exactly how it was designed to function.

Corporations have spent decades building a workplace culture where burnout is not just common but expected, where the relentless pursuit of profit outweighs any concern for human well-being. The human cost? Irrelevant. As long as the quarterly earnings report looks good, why would corporate executives care if their workforce is physically and mentally destroyed in the process?

Burnout

Burnout has been transformed into a badge of honor, and that's no accident. It's a deliberate manipulation of workers, convincing them that sacrificing their health, time, and mental well-being is not only expected but noble. You're supposed to wear your exhaustion like a medal, proof that you're dedicated enough to be a part of the "team." You're supposed to be proud of how little sleep you get, how many vacations you skip, and how many weekends you sacrifice. And who benefits from this martyrdom? Certainly not the workers.

The glorification of burnout is a tool of control, and it keeps workers tethered to a toxic cycle of overwork and undercompensation. Look at any corporate success story: behind every high-flying CEO or booming tech startup are countless workers who've been burned out and cast aside once they've served their purpose. Workers are treated like disposable cogs in a machine—just one more resource to be drained.

But what do companies get from this culture of burnout? More than just cheap labor. When workers are burned out, they are less likely to demand better pay, organize for better conditions, or question corporate policies. When people are mentally and physically exhausted, they don't have the energy to fight back. Burnout keeps workers compliant, desperate, and too worn down to rebel. That's the goal.

The Mental Health Crisis Corporations Won't Admit

Burnout isn't just a buzzword—it's a full-blown mental health crisis that corporate America refuses to acknowledge, let alone address. Anxiety, depression, and stress-related illnesses have become epidemic in modern workplaces, and companies are either silent about it or, worse, actively contribute to it. And no, the occasional "mental health day" or half-hearted HR wellness program doesn't cut it. These surface-level fixes are corporate lip service, meant to give the illusion that companies care about worker well-being, when in reality, they continue to drive their employees into the ground.

A 2020 survey by **Gallup** found that 76% of workers experience burnout on the job at least sometimes, with nearly 30% reporting that they are burned out "very often" or "always." These numbers aren't shocking—they're a direct result of the way corporations have structured the workplace. Constant deadlines, impossible expectations, shrinking staffs, and relentless pressure have all contributed to a workforce that is hanging on by a thread.

The tech industry, often held up as a symbol of innovation and progress, is one of the worst offenders when it comes to fueling burnout. Workers in Silicon Valley are notoriously overworked, with 70-hour work weeks becoming the norm and "crunch time" leading to months of non-stop work. The result? A generation of workers battling mental health issues, burnout, and, in some tragic cases, suicide. And yet, companies continue to glorify this environment, pushing the narrative that if you aren't willing to sacrifice your health for the job, you simply aren't dedicated enough.

But this isn't just a tech industry problem—it's everywhere. In healthcare, doctors and nurses are burning out at record rates, especially during the COVID-19 pandemic, which exposed just how little regard corporate-run hospitals have for the well-being of their staff. Retail workers are crushed under grueling shifts, abusive customers, and low pay, all while being told to plaster a smile on their faces for the sake of "customer service." Teachers, social workers, fast food employees—the list of burned-out workers grows every day, while the corporations they work for continue to rake in profits.

Wellness Programs and Empty Promises

Let's talk about the absolute joke that is corporate wellness programs. You've probably seen them—companies offering yoga classes, meditation apps, or mental health hotlines as if these superficial offerings are going to solve the problem. They won't. Corporate wellness programs are nothing but band-aid solutions slapped on the gaping wound that is systemic burnout.

These initiatives allow companies to pat themselves on the back for "caring" about their employees without actually addressing the root causes of burnout. It's not that workers aren't doing enough yoga—it's that they're overworked, underpaid, and constantly stressed out by an impossible workload. Offering a meditation session during lunch break won't fix that. These wellness programs exist to shift the responsibility for burnout back onto the worker, subtly suggesting that if they're struggling, it's because they aren't managing their stress well enough. Meanwhile, companies continue to pile on the work and keep wages stagnant.

The hypocrisy is staggering. Corporations that talk about "work-life balance" are often the same ones that demand 60-hour work weeks or refuse to pay their employees enough to cover basic living expenses. They'll tout mental health awareness while maintaining toxic work environments where taking time off is stigmatized, and anyone who complains about being overworked is told they "just don't have what it takes." The message is clear: You're only valuable to the company as long as you're useful, and if you burn out, there's a line of people waiting to replace you.

How Burnout Targets the Most Vulnerable

Burnout doesn't hit everyone equally. The most vulnerable workers—women, people of color, and low-wage employees—are often the ones hit the hardest. These workers are more likely to be in precarious positions, juggling multiple jobs, caring for family members, and dealing with systemic inequality in and out of the workplace. Yet they are expected to work just as hard, if not harder, than their more privileged counterparts, all while facing greater barriers to mental health care and support.

Take the retail industry as an example. Retail workers, who are disproportionately women and people of color, face brutal schedules, low pay, and little to no benefits. They are on their feet for hours, dealing with abusive customers, and constantly under pressure to meet impossible sales targets. And what do they get in return? Corporate platitudes about being "essential" workers while their employers rake in billions. During the COVID-19 pandemic, retail workers were praised as heroes, but when it came time to offer real support—higher wages, hazard pay, better benefits—corporations balked. Instead, these workers were left to burn out while the companies they worked for posted record profits.

Burnout also hits gig workers and low-wage employees harder because they lack the safety nets that higher-paid workers have. Without access to affordable healthcare, sick leave, or job security, low-wage workers are forced to keep grinding away, even when they're on the brink of collapse. If they quit or take time off, they risk losing their income entirely, something many simply cannot afford.

Meanwhile, executives and higher-level employees, the ones who preach about productivity and hustle, often have access to the resources they need to recover from burnout—therapy, extended vacations, personal assistants, you name it. The people at the top of the corporate ladder are insulated from the worst effects of burnout, leaving them free to demand even more from those below them.

Corporations Are Cashing In

Here's the truly ugly truth: burnout is profitable. Corporations have found a way to monetize the exhaustion and desperation of their workforce. By pushing employees to the breaking point, companies maximize the amount of labor they can extract without offering additional compensation. The faster workers burn out, the faster they can be replaced by a fresh crop of employees, who will go through the same cycle of overwork, burnout, and replacement.

In industries like retail and fast food, high turnover isn't a bug—it's a feature. Companies like Amazon, McDonald's, and Walmart rely on a constant churn of low-wage workers to keep costs down and profits high. These companies intentionally create environments where burnout is inevitable, knowing that they can easily replace burned-out employees with new ones. It's an endless cycle: squeeze workers dry, discard them, and bring in the next batch.

Amazon, in particular, has come under fire for its brutal work environments, where warehouse workers are expected to meet grueling productivity quotas and work in physically demanding conditions. The company's infamous "turnover machine" means that many workers don't last long in these jobs, but that's exactly how Amazon wants it. By keeping a steady flow of new, desperate workers, Amazon can avoid having to invest in the long-term well-being of its employees. Why offer better pay or safer working conditions when you can simply replace burned-out workers with new ones?

Burnout Isn't a Bug

Let's be clear: burnout isn't an accident. It's not just the unfortunate side effect of a few bad corporate policies. It's the inevitable result of a system designed to exploit workers for maximum profit. Corporations have perfected the art of pushing workers to their limits, reaping the rewards of their labor, and then discarding them when they're no longer useful. This isn't just unethical—it's deeply dangerous, both for the individual workers who suffer and for society as a whole.

The sooner we recognize that burnout is part of the corporate business model, the sooner we can start fighting back. Because as long as we allow corporations to treat workers like disposable commodities, the cycle of burnout, exploitation, and replacement will continue. And the only ones benefiting from it will be the same executives who profit from our exhaustion.

Corporate Indoctrination: Education, Media, and Consumerism

Corporate Influence in Public Education

Public education was once the cornerstone of American democracy—a space where critical thinking, independent thought, and civic responsibility were nurtured. But as funding for public schools has dried up, corporations have moved in, offering their "support" in exchange for influence. Under the guise of philanthropy, major corporations have found ways to dictate the content of education, ensuring that students emerge from the system not as free-thinking individuals, but as compliant workers ready to serve corporate interests.

One of the most glaring examples of this is the increasing presence of technology companies in schools. Corporations like **Google** and **Microsoft** provide "free" services, including classroom software, devices, and digital tools, in exchange for access to the minds of young students. While these companies present themselves as benefactors of modern education, their real aim is much more insidious—they are creating loyal users of their products from a young age. As students grow up using these platforms, they become dependent on them, ensuring a future customer base locked into the corporate ecosystem.

This invasion of corporate interests goes far beyond tech. Corporations shape everything from the subjects that are emphasized in schools to the way students are tested. STEM (Science, Technology, Engineering, and Math) subjects, which align closely with corporate needs for a tech-savvy workforce, are prioritized, while subjects like history, literature, and the arts—

which promote critical thinking, ethics, and social awareness—are increasingly marginalized.

Charter Schools and the Privatization of Education

The movement toward privatizing education through charter schools represents one of the most egregious examples of corporate encroachment into public education. While charter schools are often presented as innovative alternatives to traditional public schools, they are frequently funded by wealthy individuals and corporations with their own agendas. These private interests wield enormous influence over the curriculum, promoting values that align with their profit-driven motives rather than the public good.

The rise of charter schools coincides with the systematic underfunding of public schools, particularly in low-income areas. As public schools struggle to meet basic educational needs, charter schools—often supported by billionaires and corporations like **Walmart's Walton family**—present themselves as the saviors of education. But these schools frequently push a corporate agenda that emphasizes competition, individual achievement, and free-market ideology while downplaying the importance of collective action, social justice, and government accountability.

Meanwhile, traditional public schools, which serve the vast majority of students, are left to flounder with outdated resources, overcrowded classrooms, and insufficient funding. As public schools weaken, the push for privatization grows stronger, perpetuating a cycle that leaves the most vulnerable students with fewer opportunities while corporate interests continue to gain control over the education system.

Standardized Testing

The rise of standardized testing has further entrenched corporate influence in education. Companies like **Pearson** and **McGraw-Hill** have turned testing into a multibillion-dollar industry, shaping the way students are taught and assessed. The emphasis on testing has created a "teaching to the test" culture, where teachers are pressured to focus on rote memorization and narrow sets of skills, leaving little room for creativity, critical thinking, or the exploration of broader ideas.

This is no accident. Corporations benefit from an education system that prioritizes skills that serve their labor needs—math, reading comprehension, and technical abilities—over subjects that promote independent thought or civic engagement. Students are groomed to fit into the corporate mold, emerging from the system prepared to enter the workforce but often ill-equipped to challenge the very system that has shaped their education.

Standardized testing also serves as a convenient metric for justifying the expansion of charter schools and the privatization of education. Schools that fail to meet corporate-defined benchmarks are labeled as failing, opening the door for corporate-backed charter schools to swoop in and "save" the students—while further eroding public education in the process.

A Monopoly on Information

The media landscape has become yet another battleground for corporate domination. Once a diverse space where independent journalism thrived, the media is now dominated by a handful of massive conglomerates. Companies like **Comcast**, **Disney**, **AT&T**, and **News Corp** own the majority of news outlets, television networks, and digital platforms, controlling what information the public sees, hears, and consumes.

When only a few corporations control the majority of media, the narrative is no longer about truth or public interest—it's about protecting corporate interests. Critical journalism that exposes corporate corruption, environmental degradation, or labor abuses is pushed aside in favor of content that is safe, sanitized, and advertiser-friendly. These media giants are not in the business of informing the public—they are in the business of selling content that keeps viewers passive, distracted, and loyal to the brands that fund them.

As corporate consolidation has increased, investigative journalism has become one of the primary casualties. Newsrooms across the country have been gutted, with budgets slashed and journalists laid off. What remains is a media landscape filled with fluff, sensationalism, and shallow coverage that prioritizes entertainment over hard-hitting news. Independent voices are drowned out, and the public is left with a news cycle that rarely challenges the status quo or holds corporate and political elites accountable.

The Subtle Manipulation of Desire

It's not just the news that corporations control—it's the way we think, what we value, and how we see ourselves. Advertising has evolved from merely selling products to selling identities, lifestyles, and values that align with corporate interests. Corporations spend billions of dollars each year shaping public perception, convincing us that our happiness, success, and even our self-worth are tied to the products we buy.

This relentless barrage of advertising is not just about encouraging consumption—it's about shaping our desires and aspirations. Ads tell us that owning the latest phone, driving the newest car, or wearing the most fashionable clothes will make us happy, successful, and admired. They prey on our insecurities, convincing us that we are incomplete without their products.

Corporations have even learned to co-opt social movements, adopting the language of progressivism and social justice to sell products. We've seen companies like **Nike** and **Pepsi** wrap themselves in the rhetoric of empowerment and activism, promoting messages of racial justice, gender equality, and environmental sustainability—all while continuing to exploit labor, dodge taxes, and contribute to environmental destruction. This commodification of activism reduces meaningful movements to marketing slogans, diluting their power and turning resistance into a brand.

The Death of Independent Journalism

As corporate media continues to consolidate, independent journalism is all but extinct. Local newsrooms have been gutted, and many independent outlets that once held power to account have been bought out or shut down. Without independent journalism, we are left with a media landscape dominated by the interests of a few powerful corporations.

Investigative journalism—the kind that takes time, money, and freedom from corporate influence—has been one of the biggest casualties. Stories that could expose corporate misconduct or challenge the power structure are increasingly rare, replaced by clickbait and infotainment that keeps the public distracted and disengaged. Without a free and independent press, democracy itself is weakened, as the corporate narrative becomes the only narrative.

The Corporate Creation of Desires and Needs

Consumerism is no longer just about buying products—it's about buying identities. Corporations have mastered the art of selling more than just goods; they sell lifestyles, status, and meaning. Through relentless advertising, corporations have convinced us that consumption is not only the path to happiness but also a moral obligation. The more we consume, the more we contribute to the economy, to society, and to our personal success.

But consumerism as a new religion has sinister undertones. Corporations manipulate our desires, creating needs where none existed before. The latest gadgets, fashion trends, or diet fads aren't simply responses to consumer demand—they are manufactured by the companies that profit from them. By constantly shifting trends and creating artificial scarcity, corporations ensure that we are always chasing after the next big thing, never satisfied, always hungry for more.

This cycle of endless consumption serves to distract and pacify the public. As long as we are focused on acquiring more stuff—whether it's the latest phone, the newest car, or the most exclusive fashion—we are less likely to question the broader systems of power that control our lives. Consumerism becomes a form of control, keeping us docile and distracted while corporations continue to amass wealth and influence.

The Cult of Consumerism

In today's world, brands have become more than just products—they have become identities. People define themselves by the brands they buy, whether it's the Apple logo on their phone, the Nike swoosh on their shoes, or the Starbucks cup in their hand. This cult of consumerism has transformed shopping from a mere economic transaction into an expression of self.

Corporations have capitalized on this by positioning themselves as more than just sellers of goods. They present their brands as symbols of who we are or aspire to be. Buying a certain brand is no longer just about the product itself—it's about buying into a lifestyle, a community, a sense of belonging. But this connection to brands is artificial, built on slick marketing and carefully constructed corporate narratives.

The corporate creation of brand loyalty starts young. Children are targeted by advertising from the moment they can comprehend a screen, taught that their worth is tied to the brands they wear, the toys they own, and the shows they watch. By the time they reach adulthood, they are fully indoctrinated into the cult of consumerism, defining their identities through the brands they choose.

The Environmental and Social Costs of Consumerism

This endless cycle of consumption doesn't just have psychological costs—it has devastating environmental and social consequences. The constant push to buy more, upgrade more, and replace more has led to an explosion of waste, pollution, and environmental degradation. Corporations push products with built-in obsolescence, ensuring that they will need to be replaced within a few years, if not months.

Meanwhile, the human cost of consumerism is hidden behind supply chains that stretch across the globe. The smartphones we buy, the clothes we wear, and the food we eat are often produced by exploited workers in sweatshops or factories where labor rights are nonexistent. These workers—who are paid poverty wages and work in unsafe conditions—are the ones paying the real price for our consumer goods.

Consumerism as Control

Consumerism has become the new religion of corporate America, shaping our desires, our identities, and our values. By manipulating what we want and need, corporations have created a society where consumption is equated with success, and where the relentless pursuit of material goods distracts us from the real issues at hand. As long as we remain obedient consumers, the corporate machine will continue to grow unchecked.

Lobbying and the Corporate State

The Lobbying Industry: How Corporations Bought Washington

Corporate lobbying is not a new phenomenon, but its influence has reached unprecedented heights. In 2022 alone, over $3.7 billion was spent on lobbying in the United States, with the vast majority of that money coming from corporate interests. The lobbying industry, a vast web of well-connected professionals, former politicians, and corporate lawyers, is designed to funnel corporate money into the halls of Congress, ensuring that laws, regulations, and policies are written to benefit the bottom lines of powerful companies, not the public.

But what exactly is lobbying? On the surface, it seems harmless enough—corporations and organizations advocating for policies they support. But peel back the layers, and you'll find that lobbying is nothing short of legal bribery. Corporations pump millions of dollars into lobbying firms to ensure that their voices are the loudest in Washington. These firms hire former lawmakers and government officials, who have inside knowledge and personal relationships with sitting members of Congress. These lobbyists use their access to lawmakers to push corporate agendas, ensuring that policies favor deregulation, tax breaks, and other corporate-friendly legislation.

The results of this influence are obvious. Corporate tax rates have been slashed, environmental regulations have been gutted, and worker protections have been systematically dismantled, all thanks to the relentless pressure exerted by corporate lobbyists. The fossil fuel industry, for instance, spends billions to ensure that climate change policies are watered down or blocked entirely. Pharmaceutical companies lobby to prevent meaningful reforms to the healthcare system, keeping drug prices sky-high and their profits even higher. The financial sector, responsible for the 2008 economic collapse, lobbied heavily against new regulations in the aftermath of the crisis, ensuring that they could continue business as usual, unscathed and unpunished.

This is not how democracy is supposed to work. Theoretically, our elected officials are supposed to represent the will of the people. But in reality, they represent the will of corporations that line their pockets. Lobbyists have turned Washington into a playground for the rich and powerful, while the rest of us are left to deal with the fallout of their greed.

Corporate America's Secret Weapon

One of the most insidious ways corporations have taken over the political process is through the revolving door between government and corporate America. Here's how it works: a politician or government official spends a few years in public service, building relationships, learning the ins and outs of the legislative process, and gaining influence. Then, after leaving office, they are immediately hired by a lobbying firm or a corporation in the industry they were supposed to regulate. They use their connections and insider knowledge to push their new employer's agenda, often at the expense of the public good.

The revolving door spins both ways. Not only do former government officials land cushy jobs in the private sector, but corporate executives often take positions in government, where they have the power to directly shape policy in their company's favor. Take, for example, **Rex Tillerson**, the former CEO of **ExxonMobil**, who was appointed Secretary of State under the Trump administration. Or look at **Ajit Pai**, a former lawyer for **Verizon** who became the head of the **Federal Communications Commission (FCC)** and led the charge to repeal net neutrality, a policy that benefited corporations like Verizon at the expense of ordinary internet users.

The revolving door between government and corporate America is a blatant conflict of interest, yet it is treated as normal business in Washington. This system ensures that corporate interests are always prioritized, no matter who is in power. Lawmakers and regulators, knowing that lucrative private sector jobs await them, are incentivized to please their future employers, not the public they are supposed to serve.

Buying Elections

Lobbying is just one tool corporations use to control the political process. Campaign finance is another, and it's just as destructive. Over the years, corporations have funneled billions of dollars into political campaigns, ensuring that the candidates who win elections are beholden to their corporate backers, not to the voters. The flood of corporate money into politics has effectively silenced the voices of ordinary Americans, making it nearly impossible for working-class citizens to run for office or have their concerns heard.

The 2010 **Citizens United** decision by the Supreme Court was a turning point in the battle for political influence. The ruling declared that corporations and unions have the same free speech rights as individuals, allowing them to spend unlimited amounts of money on political campaigns. This decision opened the floodgates for corporate money to pour into elections, making it easier than ever for corporations to buy influence and shape the political landscape.

Since Citizens United, political spending has skyrocketed, with Super PACs (political action committees that can raise unlimited funds) and dark money groups (which don't have to disclose their donors) becoming major players in American elections. These organizations are funded by billionaires, corporations, and special interests, and they use their vast financial resources to shape election outcomes by flooding the airwaves with attack ads, misinformation, and propaganda. The result is a political system where candidates need corporate backing to have a chance at winning, and once in office, they are expected to return the favor.

What does this mean for the rest of us? It means that the issues that matter most to ordinary Americans—affordable healthcare, living wages, climate action—are pushed aside in favor of policies that benefit corporate donors. It means that our elected officials no longer represent us, but the wealthy elite who bankroll their campaigns. It means that democracy has been hijacked by corporate power, leaving the people voiceless in the very system that is supposed to protect their rights.

Big Pharma's Stranglehold on Healthcare Policy

Nowhere is the corrosive influence of corporate lobbying more evident than in the pharmaceutical industry. **Big Pharma** spends more on lobbying than any other industry, and they've used that money to ensure that American healthcare policy remains rigged in their favor. While millions of Americans struggle to afford life-saving medications, pharmaceutical companies rake in record profits, shielded from accountability by the politicians they've bought and paid for.

Take, for example, the fight over Medicare negotiating drug prices. For years, there has been widespread public support for allowing Medicare to negotiate with pharmaceutical companies to lower the cost of prescription drugs. This policy would save billions of dollars and make medications more affordable for millions of seniors. But Big Pharma has fought tooth and nail to prevent this from happening, spending millions on lobbying and campaign contributions to block any attempt at reform.

In 2021, despite overwhelming public support, efforts to allow Medicare to negotiate drug prices once again failed to pass in Congress. Why? Because pharmaceutical companies flooded Washington with lobbyists and campaign donations, ensuring that lawmakers—many of whom had received large sums of money from Big Pharma—would vote against the interests of their constituents. The result is a healthcare system where drug prices are the highest in the world, and millions of Americans are forced to choose between paying for their medications or paying for rent and food.

This is not an isolated incident. Big Pharma's influence extends to every aspect of healthcare policy, from preventing the importation of cheaper drugs from other countries to blocking regulations on opioid distribution, even as the opioid crisis devastated communities across America. The pharmaceutical industry's stranglehold on policy is a direct result of their massive lobbying efforts and political contributions, which have allowed them to put profits over people with little to no consequence.

A Broken Democracy

The corporate takeover of our political system has profound consequences for democracy. When corporations have more influence over lawmakers than the people they are supposed to represent, democracy ceases to function as it should. Instead of being a government of, by, and for the people, we now have a government that serves the interests of corporations and the ultra-wealthy.

This isn't just about bad policy decisions—it's about the very integrity of our political system. Corporate lobbying and campaign finance have created a political landscape where money equals power, and the voices of ordinary Americans are drowned out by corporate cash. This has led to widespread disillusionment with the political process, as more and more people feel that their votes and voices don't matter.

And they're right to feel that way. When lawmakers prioritize the interests of their corporate donors over the needs of their constituents, trust in government erodes. People begin to lose faith in the ability of the democratic system to deliver real change, and voter turnout declines. This, in turn, only strengthens the grip of corporate interests, as low voter engagement makes it easier for corporations to continue controlling the political process.

The corporate capture of democracy is a slow-moving catastrophe. It undermines the foundations of our political system, erodes public trust, and exacerbates inequality by ensuring that the rich get richer while the rest of us are left to fend for ourselves in a rigged system. As long as corporations continue to buy influence, the needs of the American people will be ignored, and democracy itself will remain under siege.

Rigged Policies That Benefit the Rich

Corporate control over the political process doesn't just undermine democracy—it has catastrophic real-world consequences for ordinary Americans. The policies that are enacted by our lawmakers, shaped by corporate lobbyists and big-money interests, have one overarching goal: to maximize profits for the few at the expense of the many. Every time a law is passed or a regulation is gutted to benefit a corporation, it is ordinary people who pay the price, often with their livelihoods, their health, or their futures.

This section will explore the devastating policy consequences of corporate domination, from economic inequality and environmental degradation to the destruction of public health and social safety nets. These policies are not accidents or unfortunate side effects—they are the direct result of a political system that has been bought and paid for by corporate America.

One of the most glaring consequences of corporate influence on government is the explosion of economic inequality in the United States. Decades of policies designed to benefit corporations and the wealthy have hollowed out the middle class and left millions of Americans struggling to make ends meet. Meanwhile, the richest Americans and the corporations they run have amassed unprecedented wealth and power, further entrenching their dominance over the political system.

Corporate tax cuts, deregulation, and anti-labor policies have all played a role in widening the gap between the haves and the have-nots. The **2017 Tax Cuts and Jobs Act**—one of the biggest legislative victories for corporate America in recent history—is a prime example of how rigged policies are designed to enrich the already wealthy while doing little to nothing for ordinary Americans.

The 2017 tax law slashed the corporate tax rate from 35% to 21%, providing a massive windfall for large companies. Proponents of the bill argued that cutting corporate taxes would lead to job creation, wage increases, and economic growth. But in reality, much of the money saved by corporations was funneled into stock buybacks, enriching executives and shareholders while workers saw little benefit. **Apple**, for example, used the savings from the tax cuts to repurchase billions of dollars' worth of its own stock, boosting its stock price and making its executives even wealthier. Meanwhile, wages for American workers remained stagnant, and income inequality continued to soar.

This isn't just a one-off case. Over the past several decades, corporate lobbying has ensured that tax policy in the United States overwhelmingly favors the wealthy and corporations, while ordinary Americans are left to pick up the tab. Loopholes in the tax code allow corporations to stash profits offshore to avoid paying taxes, while working-class Americans are taxed on every dollar they earn. The richest individuals, thanks to tax breaks on capital gains and inherited wealth, pay lower tax rates than many middle-class families. The result is an economy that is increasingly stacked against ordinary people, where the rich get richer, and the rest are left to scrape by.

The consequences of these policies are devastating. As wealth continues to concentrate in the hands of a few, the American Dream—the idea that hard work and perseverance can lead to upward mobility—has become a myth for most. Homeownership, once a cornerstone of middle-class life, is increasingly out of reach for younger generations saddled with student debt and facing stagnant wages. Retirement is no longer a certainty but a luxury few can afford, as pensions disappear and workers are forced to rely on inadequate 401(k) plans.

Economic inequality isn't just an economic issue—it's a political one. The more wealth corporations and the ultra-rich accumulate, the more power they have to influence the political process. This creates a vicious cycle, where the wealthy use their political power to enact policies that further enrich themselves, while ordinary Americans are left with less influence, less wealth, and fewer opportunities.

Profit Over Planet

Corporate control over government doesn't just lead to economic inequality—it's also destroying the planet. The fossil fuel industry, in particular, has wielded enormous political influence to block meaningful action on climate change, roll back environmental protections, and ensure that their profits continue to flow, even as the world burns. The result is a global climate crisis that threatens the very future of humanity.

For decades, fossil fuel companies have known about the dangers of climate change. Internal documents from **ExxonMobil** revealed that the company's own scientists understood the link between burning fossil fuels and global warming as far back as the 1970s. But rather than acting to mitigate the damage, Exxon and other oil companies launched a massive disinformation campaign to sow doubt about the science of climate change and block regulations that could have slowed or prevented the crisis.

These efforts were backed by billions of dollars in lobbying and campaign contributions, ensuring that politicians—many of whom were funded by the fossil fuel industry—would not take action to address climate change. The result? Decades of inaction, as the planet hurtles toward catastrophe. Even today, as wildfires rage, hurricanes intensify, and sea levels rise, the fossil fuel industry continues to pour money into lobbying efforts designed to prevent meaningful climate action.

The **American Petroleum Institute (API)**, the largest trade association for the oil and gas industry, spends millions each year lobbying against climate regulations, promoting fossil fuel expansion, and ensuring that environmental protections are weakened or eliminated. These efforts have paid off handsomely for the industry. In 2020, despite growing public awareness of the climate crisis, the Trump administration rolled back over 100 environmental regulations, many of which were put in place to reduce greenhouse gas emissions and protect public health. These rollbacks included weakening fuel efficiency standards for cars, allowing oil drilling in sensitive areas like the Arctic National Wildlife Refuge, and reducing protections for wetlands and waterways.

But it's not just fossil fuel companies that have used their political power to prioritize profits over the planet. The **chemical**, **mining**, and **agribusiness** industries have also used their influence to weaken environmental protections and avoid accountability for the pollution they cause. These industries, through aggressive lobbying efforts, have ensured that regulations meant to protect public health and the environment are watered down, delayed, or outright blocked.

For example, the **American Chemistry Council** has spent millions lobbying against efforts to regulate toxic chemicals like **PFAS**, a group of man-made chemicals linked to cancer, birth defects, and other serious health problems. Despite mounting evidence of the dangers posed by PFAS, the chemical industry has successfully delayed regulatory action, leaving millions of Americans exposed to contaminated water and soil.

The consequences of this corporate capture of environmental policy are dire. Climate change is already causing devastating impacts around the world, from extreme weather events to food shortages and mass displacement. Without immediate and drastic action, these impacts will only worsen, leading to untold suffering and loss of life. But as long as corporations continue to buy influence in Washington, meaningful action on climate change will remain out of reach, and the planet will continue to spiral toward disaster.

Big Pharma, Big Tobacco, and Corporate Greed

Another area where corporate influence has had disastrous consequences is public health. Whether it's Big Pharma manipulating drug prices, Big Tobacco delaying action on smoking-related illnesses, or the food and beverage industry fighting regulations on unhealthy products, corporate America has consistently put profits over the health and well-being of the American people.

The pharmaceutical industry's stranglehold on healthcare policy is one of the most egregious examples of corporate greed endangering public health. As we discussed in the previous section, Big Pharma spends billions each year lobbying against reforms that would lower drug prices, expand access to healthcare, and hold pharmaceutical companies accountable for their role in public health crises like the opioid epidemic.

The opioid crisis, which has claimed hundreds of thousands of lives in the United States, is a direct result of corporate malfeasance. **Purdue Pharma**, the maker of **OxyContin**, aggressively marketed its highly addictive painkillers while downplaying the risks of addiction. The company's executives and sales representatives incentivized doctors to prescribe higher doses of opioids, leading to widespread misuse and addiction. Purdue, along with other pharmaceutical companies, lobbied against efforts to regulate opioid prescriptions, ensuring that the crisis would continue to worsen.

But Purdue Pharma isn't the only corporation responsible for public health disasters. The tobacco industry has a long history of using its political influence to delay action on smoking-related illnesses. For decades, tobacco companies like **Philip Morris** and **R.J. Reynolds** funded misleading research, lobbied against regulations, and fought public health campaigns designed to reduce smoking rates. It wasn't until the 1990s that the full extent of the industry's deception was exposed, but by then, millions of lives had already been lost to smoking-related illnesses.

Today, the food and beverage industry is following in the footsteps of Big Tobacco, fighting against regulations that would curb the consumption of unhealthy products. Corporations like **Coca-Cola** and **PepsiCo** spend millions lobbying against sugar taxes, nutrition labeling, and restrictions on junk food advertising, all while promoting products that contribute to the nation's obesity and diabetes epidemics.

The pattern is clear: when corporate profits are at stake, public health takes a back seat. Whether it's pushing addictive opioids, downplaying the risks of smoking, or flooding the market with unhealthy foods, corporations have shown time and time again that they are **The Price We Pay**

The policy consequences of corporate domination are clear: growing economic inequality, environmental destruction, and a public health crisis that shows no signs of slowing down. These outcomes are not accidents—they are the direct result of a political system that prioritizes corporate profits over the needs and well-being of ordinary Americans. Every tax cut for the wealthy, every regulation rolled back, and every public health crisis ignored is another example of how corporate America has bought our democracy and made our lives worse in the process.

Until we confront the reality of corporate influence in our government, these problems will only get worse. The American people deserve better than a system rigged against them, but as long as corporations continue to pull the strings in Washington, real change will remain out of reach.

Profit Over Lives

When corporations talk about "freedom" or "efficiency," what they really mean is stripping away protections, benefits, and safety nets that allow ordinary people to survive. Over the last several decades, corporate lobbying has systematically dismantled social welfare programs, leaving millions of Americans more vulnerable than ever. It's not just an attack on the poor—it's an assault on anyone who dares to rely on something other than corporate largesse for their well-being. The message is clear: in corporate America, you're on your own.

Corporations have worked tirelessly to reduce their obligations to workers and communities while funneling public money into their own pockets. Welfare programs, once designed to provide a safety net for society's most vulnerable, have been gutted, demonized, and turned into corporate slush funds. Meanwhile, politicians, beholden to their corporate donors, have sold out the very people they are supposed to represent.

This section dives into how corporations have attacked social safety nets—from healthcare to unemployment benefits to housing—and how these efforts have led to unprecedented levels of inequality, poverty, and insecurity in the richest country on earth. This isn't just incompetence or bureaucratic inefficiency. It's by design. Corporations have rigged the system to ensure that the public is more dependent on them than ever, while the programs meant to protect ordinary people crumble.

No area of social welfare has been more ruthlessly targeted by corporate America than healthcare. In a system where health is treated as a commodity rather than a human right, the insurance and pharmaceutical industries have amassed enormous power, using that power to shape healthcare policy to maximize profits at the expense of human lives.

The United States spends more on healthcare than any other developed nation, yet millions of Americans are uninsured or underinsured, unable to afford basic medical care. How is it possible that a country with so much wealth has such a broken healthcare system? It's simple: **Big Insurance** and **Big Pharma** have bought the system, ensuring that healthcare remains unaffordable for many while they rake in obscene profits.

Lobbying by the healthcare industry has ensured that meaningful reforms are dead on arrival. The push for a **single-payer healthcare system**, or "Medicare for All," has been a consistent target of corporate attacks. The idea of providing universal healthcare terrifies the insurance and pharmaceutical industries because it would cut into their profits, so they spend millions to lobby against it, flood the airwaves with scare tactics, and fund politicians willing to uphold the status quo. The result? Americans are stuck with a privatized healthcare system where insurance companies can charge astronomical premiums, deny coverage, and force people into bankruptcy over medical bills.

One of the most grotesque examples of this influence came during the debate over the **Affordable Care Act (ACA)**. While the ACA was a step toward expanding coverage, it was a heavily compromised piece of legislation, largely due to the enormous lobbying power of insurance companies. Instead of moving toward a universal healthcare system, the ACA maintained the private insurance market, allowing corporations to continue profiting off people's illnesses. Worse yet, attempts to expand the ACA or implement public options are consistently blocked or watered down, ensuring that corporate profits remain secure while Americans suffer.

The pharmaceutical industry is equally complicit in this racket. **Big Pharma** spends more on lobbying than any other industry, and they use that influence to keep drug prices sky-high. While the rest of the world pays reasonable prices for life-saving medications, Americans are charged exorbitant rates because our government has been bought and paid for by pharmaceutical companies. Take **insulin**, for example—a drug that was discovered nearly a century ago, with its patent essentially gifted to humanity. And yet, in America, people are dying because they can't afford it, while drug companies like **Eli Lilly** rake in billions.

This isn't a system that's broken by accident; it's a system that has been designed to prioritize profit over people. Every time healthcare reform is proposed, lobbyists from the insurance and pharmaceutical industries descend on Washington to ensure that their profits are protected, even if it means Americans continue to die from preventable diseases, untreated conditions, and lack of access to affordable care.

Punishing the Most Vulnerable

In corporate America, being unemployed isn't just a financial hardship—it's a moral failing. For decades, corporations have lobbied to reduce unemployment benefits, arguing that these programs create a "culture of dependency" and discourage people from working. What they really mean is that they want a workforce so desperate for a paycheck that they'll accept any conditions, no matter how exploitative. The war on unemployment benefits is nothing short of a war on workers' dignity and rights.

After the **Great Recession** in 2008, millions of Americans lost their jobs. In a functioning society, this would have been a wake-up call to strengthen social safety nets and provide robust unemployment benefits to help people survive while they searched for new employment. Instead, what we got was a concerted effort by corporate interests to slash those benefits and force people back into the labor market as quickly as possible, regardless of the quality of the jobs available.

Corporate America has consistently lobbied to keep unemployment benefits as low as possible. States like **Florida** and **North Carolina**—both under heavy corporate influence—reduced the duration and amount of unemployment benefits available, forcing workers to take jobs well below their skill levels or for significantly lower pay. The argument pushed by corporate lobbyists is that generous unemployment benefits discourage people from seeking work. But this ignores the reality of the labor market: many of the jobs available are low-wage, part-time, and offer no benefits or job security. The attack on unemployment benefits is nothing more than an attempt to coerce workers into accepting any job, no matter how degrading or exploitative.

The **COVID-19 pandemic** exposed just how deep the corporate disdain for social safety nets goes. In the early days of the pandemic, when millions were suddenly unemployed, there was a temporary expansion of unemployment benefits under the CARES Act. For a brief moment, it seemed like the government might finally prioritize the well-being of its citizens. But that moment was short-lived. As soon as the immediate crisis began to subside, corporate America ramped up its lobbying efforts to end those benefits as quickly as possible.

Businesses, especially in low-wage industries like fast food and retail, complained that they couldn't find workers because unemployment benefits were "too generous." The reality was that workers were simply unwilling to risk their lives for poverty wages during a pandemic. But instead of raising wages or improving working conditions, corporations lobbied for the end of expanded unemployment benefits, forcing people back into unsafe jobs with little regard for their health or well-being.

This is the corporate vision for America: a workforce that is constantly on the edge of desperation, where unemployment benefits are so meager that workers have no choice but to accept whatever job is available, no matter how exploitative or dangerous. This isn't about incentivizing work—it's about controlling workers and keeping them compliant.

Gentrification, Rent Gouging, and Homelessness

Corporate greed has also played a central role in America's housing crisis. As affordable housing becomes increasingly scarce, millions of Americans are being priced out of their homes, forced to live in overcrowded conditions, or pushed into homelessness. At the same time, corporations and wealthy investors are profiting from gentrification, rent gouging, and housing speculation, turning housing—a basic human need—into a commodity for profit.

The housing crisis didn't happen by accident. It's the result of decades of lobbying by real estate developers, landlords, and financial institutions who have manipulated housing policy to benefit themselves. Rent control measures, which once protected tenants from exorbitant rent increases, have been gutted in cities across the country, thanks to aggressive lobbying by the real estate industry. In states like **California** and **New York**, where housing costs are sky-high, corporate landlords have fought tooth and nail to prevent rent control reforms, ensuring that rents continue to soar while ordinary people are priced out of their neighborhoods.

Meanwhile, private equity firms and wealthy investors have turned housing into a speculative asset, buying up homes, apartment buildings, and entire neighborhoods, driving up prices and pushing working-class families out. Corporations like **Blackstone** have become some of the largest landlords in the country, using their wealth and political influence to further deregulate the housing market, making it easier for them to exploit tenants and squeeze profits out of every square foot of housing.

Gentrification, once a localized issue, has now become a nationwide phenomenon, as corporate developers target working-class neighborhoods for "revitalization." In practice, this means displacing long-term residents, bulldozing affordable housing, and replacing it with luxury apartments, trendy coffee shops, and expensive boutiques that cater to the wealthy. The people who made these neighborhoods vibrant and unique are forced out, their homes and communities destroyed, all for the sake of corporate profit.

The result of these policies is a housing market that works only for the rich. Homeownership, once the cornerstone of the American Dream, is now out of reach for millions of Americans, particularly younger generations. Rents have skyrocketed, and even middle-class families are finding it harder and harder to afford decent housing. Meanwhile, homelessness has become a crisis in cities across the country, with tent encampments and shelters overflowing as the government fails to address the root causes of the housing crisis.

Corporate landlords, real estate developers, and financial institutions have all profited handsomely from the destruction of affordable housing. And as long as they continue to lobby against rent control, housing subsidies, and affordable housing initiatives, the crisis will only get worse. In their world, housing is not a right—it's a commodity, and the more desperate people are, the more they can charge.

Demonizing the Poor

Corporate America has also waged a decades-long war on welfare programs designed to help the most vulnerable members of society. Programs like **SNAP** (food stamps), **Medicaid**, and **Temporary Assistance for Needy Families (TANF)** have been under relentless attack, with corporate-backed politicians portraying them as wasteful and encouraging "dependency."

This narrative, pushed by corporations and their political allies, is designed to justify cutting benefits and shrinking the welfare state. But the reality is that these programs are lifelines for millions of Americans who would otherwise be left to fend for themselves in an economy that increasingly leaves them behind. Instead of addressing the systemic issues that cause poverty—like stagnant wages, skyrocketing healthcare costs, and a lack of affordable housing—corporations and politicians demonize the poor, blaming them for their own circumstances.

The attacks on welfare have real consequences. In 1996, under President Bill Clinton, **TANF** replaced **Aid to Families with Dependent Children (AFDC)**, drastically cutting welfare benefits and placing strict work requirements on recipients. The result has been an explosion of extreme poverty, with millions of families forced to live on less than $2 a day. Despite the obvious failure of this approach, corporate-backed politicians continue to push for further cuts to welfare programs, insisting that people should "pull themselves up by their bootstraps"—even as the system is rigged against them.

The truth is that welfare programs don't create dependency—they provide a safety net for people who are struggling to survive in an economy dominated by corporate interests. But as long as corporations control the narrative, welfare programs will continue to be demonized, and the poor will continue to be scapegoated for problems that are the result of corporate greed and political corruption.

The System Is Rigged, and We're Paying the Price

The erosion of social welfare programs is not the result of economic necessity or government inefficiency—it's the result of corporate lobbying and a political system that prioritizes profits over people. From healthcare to housing to unemployment benefits, corporations have worked tirelessly to dismantle the safety nets that protect ordinary Americans, ensuring that we are more dependent on them than ever before.

This is the true cost of corporate domination: a society where the most vulnerable are left to fend for themselves, where basic human needs are commodified and exploited for profit, and where the American Dream has been reduced to a cruel joke. The system is rigged, and we're all paying the price.

It doesn't have to be this way. But until we confront the power that corporations wield over our government, our economy, and our lives, nothing will change. Corporate America has made it clear that they will continue to strip away our rights, our protections, and our dignity—unless we fight back.

Labor Movements and the Fight for Workers' Rights

A Brief History of Labor Movements

Corporate America's relentless drive for profit has come at the expense of workers' rights, safety, and dignity. Over the past several decades, corporations have used every tool at their disposal to strip workers of their ability to organize, negotiate, and fight for fair treatment. Labor unions, once a powerful force in American society, have been systematically weakened and vilified, while workers are left to fend for themselves in an economy that treats them as disposable.

But here's the truth: the only thing that has ever stood between corporate greed and total domination is the labor movement. The fight for workers' rights has always been a fight against corporate power, and despite the relentless attacks, it's a fight that continues today. In this section, we'll dive into the history of the labor movement, examine the corporate assault on unions, and explore how workers are rising up once again to demand fair wages, safe working conditions, and basic human dignity.\

To understand the current state of the labor movement, we must first understand its roots. The labor movement in America has always been a story of workers coming together to resist exploitation, organize for collective bargaining, and demand better treatment from the ruling elite. In the late 19th and early 20th centuries, American workers faced brutal conditions: long hours, low pay, and dangerous workplaces where injury or death was a constant risk. Corporations operated with near-total impunity, exploiting workers to maximize profits while offering little in return.

In response to these conditions, workers began to organize. Early labor unions like the **Knights of Labor** and the **American Federation of Labor (AFL)** emerged as powerful forces in the fight for workers' rights, advocating for shorter workdays, better wages, and safer working conditions. Through strikes, protests, and organizing efforts, these unions made significant gains, forcing corporations to negotiate with workers and securing many of the labor protections we take for granted today: the 40-hour workweek, the minimum wage, child labor laws, and workplace safety regulations.

But these gains were not won without a fight. The history of labor in America is stained with blood—corporate America has always fought tooth and nail to keep workers under its heel. From the **Pullman Strike** of 1894, where federal troops were sent to break up a railroad workers' strike, to the **Ludlow Massacre** of 1914, where striking coal miners and their families were slaughtered by the Colorado National Guard, the labor movement has faced brutal opposition from both corporations and the government. Workers have been beaten, arrested, and even killed for daring to demand better treatment.

Despite these challenges, the labor movement persisted, and by the mid-20th century, labor unions were at the height of their power. The rise of industrial unions like the **United Auto Workers (UAW)** and the **International Brotherhood of Teamsters** gave workers in key industries the ability to negotiate for better wages, benefits, and working conditions. The post-World War II economic boom was, in large part, the result of these hard-won gains, as unionized workers were able to secure a share of the wealth they helped create.

But corporate America never forgot those early losses. And by the late 20th century, they were ready to strike back.

The Corporate Assault on Unions

The decline of labor unions in America wasn't a natural process—it was a deliberate, calculated attack orchestrated by corporate interests determined to strip workers of their power. Starting in the 1970s, corporations launched an all-out assault on unions, using their political and economic power to weaken labor laws, undermine organizing efforts, and erode the hard-won rights of American workers.

One of the most significant blows to the labor movement came with the rise of **neoliberalism**, an economic ideology that prioritized free markets, deregulation, and the erosion of government protections for workers. Neoliberalism, championed by political leaders like **Ronald Reagan** in the United States and **Margaret Thatcher** in the UK, painted unions as an obstacle to economic growth, portraying them as corrupt, inefficient, and anti-business. This rhetoric was a smokescreen, designed to convince the public that unions—rather than corporations—were responsible for the economic struggles of the time.

In reality, the corporate assault on unions was about one thing: profit. By dismantling unions, corporations could drive down wages, eliminate benefits, and increase profits without fear of organized resistance. And they were wildly successful. In 1981, President Reagan's decision to fire over 11,000 striking air traffic controllers during the **PATCO strike** signaled the beginning of a new era of corporate power. The message was clear: the government would no longer support workers' right to strike, and corporations could crush unions with impunity.

Following the PATCO strike, corporations ramped up their efforts to weaken unions, using tactics like outsourcing, offshoring, and automation to reduce the power of organized labor. Manufacturing jobs, once the backbone of the American middle class, were shipped overseas to countries where labor was cheaper, and workers had fewer rights. Union-busting became a multi-billion-dollar industry, with law firms and consulting companies specializing in preventing workers from organizing and breaking up unions that already existed.

At the same time, corporate lobbyists worked tirelessly to erode labor protections at the federal and state levels. **"Right-to-work" laws**, which allow workers to opt out of paying union dues while still benefiting from union-negotiated contracts, were passed in states across the country, severely weakening unions' ability to collect funds and maintain solidarity. These laws, pushed by corporate interests, were sold to the public as pro-worker measures, but their real goal was to divide workers and undermine collective bargaining power.

The results of these efforts have been devastating for American workers. In the 1950s, nearly a third of the American workforce was unionized. Today, that number has fallen to just over 10%, and in the private sector, it's less than 7%. As union membership has declined, so too have wages, benefits, and job security. The middle class—once the foundation of the American economy—has been hollowed out, while corporate profits have soared to record levels. This is not a coincidence; it is the direct result of a deliberate, decades-long campaign to crush the labor movement and transfer wealth from workers to the corporate elite.

A New Form of Exploitation

As unions have weakened, corporations have found new ways to exploit workers. The rise of the **gig economy** represents the latest frontier in the corporate war on labor, where workers are classified as independent contractors rather than employees, allowing companies to avoid providing basic benefits and protections. Companies like **Uber**, **Lyft**, and **DoorDash** have built multi-billion-dollar empires on the backs of gig workers who have no access to healthcare, no job security, and no right to unionize.

The gig economy has been sold to the public as a source of freedom and flexibility, where workers can "be their own boss" and choose their own hours. But this narrative is a lie. In reality, gig workers are at the mercy of corporate algorithms that determine when and where they can work, how much they will be paid, and whether they will even have access to the platform. They are constantly underpaid, overworked, and exploited, with no recourse for grievances or injustices.

Gig workers are not the only ones suffering under this new model of exploitation. The rise of contract work, part-time work, and precarious employment has spread across industries, as corporations seek to reduce labor costs by eliminating full-time jobs with benefits. Workers in industries ranging from tech to education to healthcare are increasingly being classified as independent contractors, freelancers, or temporary workers, stripping them of the protections that full-time employees enjoy.

The gig economy is nothing more than a modern version of the same exploitative labor practices that unions fought against in the early 20th century. But this time, corporations have learned to package it in a way that seems innovative and progressive, using buzzwords like "flexibility" and "entrepreneurship" to disguise what is, at its core, a system of worker exploitation.

Workers Fighting Back

Despite the relentless assault on unions and workers' rights, there are signs of hope. In recent years, a new wave of labor activism has begun to rise, as workers across industries organize, strike, and fight back against corporate exploitation. This resurgence of labor is a direct response to the growing inequality, insecurity, and injustice that have come to define the American economy.

One of the most visible examples of this new labor movement is the fight for a **$15 minimum wage**. Fast food workers, organized under the banner of the **Fight for $15**, have led strikes and protests across the country, demanding fair wages and the right to unionize. While the federal minimum wage has remained stagnant at $7.25 for over a decade, these efforts have led to significant victories at the state and local levels, with cities like **Seattle** and **New York** adopting a $15 minimum wage.

The resurgence of labor isn't limited to fast food workers. Teachers, nurses, warehouse workers, and tech employees have all begun to organize and strike for better wages, working conditions, and benefits. In 2018, teachers in **West Virginia** led a statewide strike, demanding higher pay and better healthcare benefits. Their strike, which was initially illegal under state law, inspired a wave of teacher strikes across the country, from **Oklahoma** to **Arizona** to **Los Angeles**. These strikes were not just about wages—they were about fighting back against a system that has consistently underfunded public education while enriching corporations and the wealthy.

Tech workers, long seen as isolated from the struggles of traditional labor, have also begun to organize in response to corporate abuses. Employees at companies like **Google**, **Amazon**, and **Microsoft** have staged walkouts and protests over issues ranging from workplace harassment to unethical business practices, demanding that their employers prioritize human rights and employee welfare over profits.

Warehouse workers at **Amazon**, one of the most notoriously exploitative companies in the country, have also begun to fight back. In **Bessemer, Alabama**, Amazon workers made national headlines with their effort to unionize in 2021, a historic attempt to challenge the company's brutal working conditions, where employees are forced to work at breakneck speeds, denied bathroom breaks, and treated like cogs in a machine. Although the union vote ultimately failed after a vicious anti-union campaign by Amazon, the effort was a powerful signal that workers are no longer willing to accept corporate abuse without a fight.

Organizing for Power

The resurgence of labor is a reminder that the fight for workers' rights is far from over. Despite the corporate stranglehold on government, the media, and the economy, workers are organizing, striking, and demanding their fair share of the wealth they create. The labor movement, once dismissed as a relic of the past, is proving that it is still a powerful force in the fight against corporate greed.

But the future of labor depends on our ability to continue organizing, building solidarity, and fighting back against the forces that seek to divide and conquer us. The fight for workers' rights is not just about higher wages or better benefits—it's about reclaiming power from corporations that have rigged the system against us.

The only way to counter the power of corporate America is through collective action. As workers, we must organize, strike, and demand more from our employers, our government, and our economy. We must rebuild the labor movement, strengthen unions, and support new forms of organizing that can adapt to the challenges of the modern economy. This isn't just a fight for workers' rights—it's a fight for democracy itself, a fight to ensure that power remains in the hands of the people, not the corporations.

Taking Back Our Neighborhoods

The fight against corporate control isn't limited to labor unions—it extends deep into communities where grassroots resistance is building momentum against the forces that have been destroying neighborhoods, disenfranchising citizens, and robbing people of their power. Corporations have spent decades infiltrating local governments, eroding public services, and dictating policy to serve their own interests. But across the country, individuals and communities are standing up and fighting back. They're organizing from the ground up, refusing to be complicit in a system that prioritizes profit over people.

Community organizing is about reclaiming power on the most fundamental level: where people live, work, and connect. It's about dismantling the corporate structures that have devastated our environment, siphoned off resources, and stripped away the safety nets that once supported ordinary Americans. And it's about restoring power to the hands of the people who are directly affected by corporate greed. This section will explore the resurgence of grassroots organizing, how communities are banding together to resist corporate control, and the ways in which local actions are challenging systemic power.

One of the most visible ways that corporate greed has reshaped our communities is through gentrification—a process that strips neighborhoods of their identity, displaces long-term residents, and replaces them with sterile, high-rent developments designed to attract wealthier, often whiter, populations. Gentrification isn't just about rising rents or trendy coffee shops; it's about corporations and developers seizing control of entire neighborhoods, turning them into profit centers while erasing the history and culture of the people who built those communities.

For decades, real estate developers, corporate landlords, and financial institutions have preyed on working-class neighborhoods, buying up properties, hiking rents, and forcing people out of their homes. In cities like **San Francisco**, **New York**, and **Los Angeles**, entire communities have been uprooted as tech companies and real estate speculators drive housing prices into the stratosphere. The people who lived in these neighborhoods for generations—often Black, Latino, and immigrant communities—are pushed out, while developers move in and transform their homes into luxury condos and boutique hotels.

But across the country, communities are fighting back. In cities like **Detroit**, **Oakland**, and **Washington, D.C.**, grassroots movements have sprung up to resist gentrification and reclaim neighborhoods from corporate interests. These movements are demanding rent control, affordable housing, and protections for tenants facing displacement. They are organizing tenants' unions, staging rent strikes, and putting pressure on local governments to pass anti-gentrification laws.

For example, in **Oakland**, the fight against gentrification has become a rallying cry for a diverse coalition of activists, community organizers, and residents who refuse to let their neighborhoods be sold to the highest bidder. Groups like the **Alliance of Californians for Community Empowerment (ACCE)** have led efforts to pass rent control measures, prevent evictions, and hold corporate landlords accountable for predatory practices. These movements recognize that housing is a human right, and they are fighting to ensure that working-class people have a place in the cities they helped build.

In **New York City**, tenant organizing has a long and storied history, but in recent years it has gained new urgency as corporate landlords continue to displace residents in favor of high-rent developments. Tenant unions and advocacy groups like **Right to the City** and **Make the Road New York** have led campaigns to fight back against evictions, demand stronger rent control laws, and push for more affordable housing. In 2019, these efforts culminated in a major victory with the passage of the **Housing Stability and Tenant Protection Act**, which strengthened rent protections for millions of New Yorkers. This victory was a direct result of grassroots organizing and pressure from tenants and advocates who refused to be silenced by the overwhelming power of real estate developers and corporate landlords.

These examples show that gentrification, while a formidable force, is not inevitable. Communities can and are fighting back, reclaiming their neighborhoods from corporate interests and building power from the ground up. These fights are not just about housing—they're about dignity, justice, and the right to remain in the places that people call home.

Environmental Justice

Another area where grassroots resistance is taking shape is in the fight for environmental justice. For decades, corporations have treated marginalized communities—particularly Black, Indigenous, and low-income communities—as dumping grounds for pollution, toxic waste, and industrial development. The result has been devastating: communities of color and poor neighborhoods bear the brunt of environmental degradation, suffering from higher rates of asthma, cancer, and other diseases caused by corporate negligence.

But in recent years, these communities have begun to organize, fighting back against the corporations that pollute their air, water, and land. The **environmental justice** movement, led by activists and organizers from the most affected communities, is demanding accountability from the industries that have poisoned their neighborhoods and calling for policies that protect human health and the environment over corporate profits.

One of the most high-profile battles in the fight for environmental justice took place in **Flint, Michigan**, where residents—predominantly low-income and Black—were exposed to toxic levels of lead in their drinking water after the state government, under pressure from corporate interests, decided to switch the city's water supply to save money. For years, residents complained about the water's foul smell, taste, and discoloration, but their concerns were dismissed by local officials, who downplayed the crisis and failed to act.

It wasn't until activists, led by Flint residents themselves, began to organize and bring attention to the crisis that the true extent of the contamination was exposed. Grassroots groups like **Water You Fighting For** and **Flint Rising** mobilized the community, held protests, and demanded answers from government officials and corporations. Their efforts brought national attention to the crisis, forcing the government to admit wrongdoing and take steps to address the water contamination. While the fight for justice in Flint is far from over, the activism of

Flint residents has sparked a larger movement for water rights and environmental justice across the country.

Another powerful example of environmental justice organizing can be seen in the **Standing Rock Sioux Tribe's** resistance to the **Dakota Access Pipeline (DAPL)**. For months, Indigenous activists, water protectors, and allies camped out at Standing Rock, resisting the construction of an oil pipeline that threatened their water supply and sacred lands. Despite brutal repression by law enforcement and private security forces hired by the pipeline company, the Standing Rock movement captured the world's attention, inspiring solidarity actions across the globe.

The resistance at Standing Rock was about more than just a pipeline—it was about Indigenous sovereignty, environmental justice, and the right of communities to protect their land and water from corporate exploitation. While the pipeline was eventually completed, the movement galvanized a new generation of environmental activists and sparked a wave of Indigenous-led resistance to extractive industries across North America.

These fights for environmental justice are part of a broader movement to hold corporations accountable for the damage they have done to marginalized communities. From urban neighborhoods plagued by industrial pollution to rural areas facing the destruction of natural resources, grassroots movements are pushing back against corporate power and demanding justice for the communities that have been treated as expendable.

Political Organizing

Grassroots organizing isn't just about fighting corporations—it's about building political power to challenge the system that enables corporate dominance. Across the country, community organizers and activists are working to elect candidates who are accountable to the people, not corporate donors, and to pass laws that protect workers, the environment, and civil rights.

One of the most significant examples of grassroots political organizing in recent years is the rise of the **Democratic Socialists of America (DSA)**, which has grown rapidly in response to widespread disillusionment with the corporate-controlled political system. The DSA has helped elect progressive candidates like **Alexandria Ocasio-Cortez and Cori Bush**, who have become powerful voices for working-class people in Congress, pushing for policies like Medicare for All, the Green New Deal, and criminal justice reform.

But the DSA's work goes beyond electoral politics. It's about building a movement from the ground up, organizing tenants, workers, and students to fight for systemic change. In cities across the country, DSA chapters are organizing mutual aid networks, supporting labor strikes, and advocating for housing justice, showing that grassroots power can effect real change even in the face of overwhelming corporate influence.

Another powerful example of grassroots political organizing is the fight for voting rights. Across the United States, particularly in Republican-controlled states, there has been a concerted effort to roll back voting rights through voter suppression laws aimed at disenfranchising Black, Latino, and low-income voters. But in response, grassroots organizations like **Fair Fight Action**, founded by **Stacey Abrams**, have mobilized to protect voting rights, register new voters, and fight back against voter suppression.

In **Georgia**, Fair Fight Action played a crucial role in flipping the state in the 2020 presidential election, registering hundreds of thousands of new voters and organizing efforts to ensure that people were able to vote despite the obstacles put in place by Republican lawmakers. This kind of grassroots organizing is essential to countering the power of corporate-backed politicians who rely on voter suppression to maintain control.

Grassroots political movements are not just about electing the right candidates—they're about building power from the ground up, creating networks of support, and fostering a culture of resistance to corporate control. These movements recognize that the only way to challenge the entrenched power of corporations is by organizing in our communities, standing in solidarity with one another, and building a political system that works for the people, not the wealthy elite.

Building Solidarity Across Struggles

One of the most powerful aspects of community organizing is the way it builds solidarity across struggles. The fight against corporate control isn't limited to any one issue—it's about recognizing the interconnectedness of our struggles and standing together in the face of a system that thrives on division and exploitation.

Environmental justice, housing rights, labor organizing, and political action are not separate fights—they are all part of the same broader movement to reclaim power from the corporations that have rigged the system against us. Grassroots movements understand this, and they are building coalitions that cut across issues, recognizing that real change will only come when we stand united against the forces of greed and exploitation.

In **Chicago**, for example, the **Chicago Teachers Union (CTU)** has been at the forefront of a movement that goes beyond traditional labor organizing. The CTU has fought not only for better wages and working conditions for teachers but also for broader social justice issues like affordable housing, healthcare, and racial equity. By building coalitions with community organizations, tenants' rights groups, and healthcare advocates, the CTU has shown that the fight for workers' rights is inseparable from the fight for social justice.

This kind of solidarity is essential to building a movement capable of challenging corporate power. Corporations rely on division to maintain control—they pit workers against each other, stoke racial and economic tensions, and sow fear to keep people divided and disorganized. But grassroots movements understand that our struggles are interconnected, and they are building the kind of solidarity that can break down those barriers and create a united front against corporate domination.

Grassroots Power Is the Key to Change

The fight against corporate control will not be won in boardrooms or through backroom deals—it will be won in the streets, in our communities, and through the power of grassroots organizing. From tenant unions to environmental justice movements to political campaigns, ordinary people are standing up, organizing, and fighting back against the system that has exploited them for far too long.

Community organizing is about more than just resisting—it's about building power. It's about reclaiming our neighborhoods, protecting our environment, and ensuring that our political system works for the many, not the few. The corporate elite may have money, but we have people—and when people organize, they can achieve incredible things.

Reclaiming Our Democracy from Corporate Cash

The stranglehold that corporations have on our government, economy, and society can feel insurmountable. Their influence has infiltrated every corner of American life, from the laws that shape our working conditions to the media we consume. But if history has taught us anything, it's that no power is absolute, and corporate America is not invincible. With strategic policy reforms, mass movements, and collective action, we can begin to dismantle the corporate state and rebuild a society that puts people before profits.

This section explores how we can push for policy reforms that challenge corporate power, strengthen democratic institutions, and protect workers, the environment, and public health. But policy alone won't solve the problem—real change requires a groundswell of collective action. From voting rights and campaign finance reform to pushing corporations to pay their fair share of taxes, the fight for reform is a fight for democracy itself.

The single greatest tool that corporations use to maintain their power over our political system is money. **Campaign finance** is the engine that drives corporate influence in Washington and in state legislatures across the country. Without serious reform to how elections are funded, any attempts to curb corporate power will be meaningless, as politicians will continue to prioritize the interests of the corporations that bankroll their campaigns over the needs of ordinary people.

One of the most significant barriers to campaign finance reform is the **Citizens United v. FEC** decision, which opened the floodgates for unlimited corporate spending in politics. Since that ruling, corporations and billionaires have been able to pour billions into Super PACs and dark money groups, effectively buying elections and ensuring that their interests dominate the political landscape. Citizens United turned our democracy into a marketplace, where the loudest voices are the ones with the deepest pockets.

To reclaim our democracy, we must overturn Citizens United and implement comprehensive campaign finance reforms that limit the influence of corporate money in politics. This means pushing for constitutional amendments that redefine political spending as a regulated activity, subject to strict oversight. Public financing of elections is another crucial reform, ensuring that candidates can run viable campaigns without relying on corporate donations. States like **Maine** and **Arizona** have already implemented public financing models, allowing candidates to focus on voters, not donors.

In addition to overturning Citizens United, we need transparency in political spending. Dark money—political spending by organizations that don't have to disclose their donors—must be exposed. Passing laws like the **DISCLOSE Act**, which would require organizations to reveal the sources of their funding, is a crucial step in shedding light on who is really influencing our elections. The American people deserve to know who is buying their politicians, and without that transparency, corporate influence will continue to corrupt the political process.

Beyond campaign finance, there is also a need for **lobbying reform**. Corporations spend billions every year on lobbying to manipulate legislation and regulation to their advantage. We must place stricter limits on lobbying, especially the kind of **revolving door** politics that allow former government officials to take high-paying lobbying jobs with industries they used to regulate. Banning this practice and enacting mandatory cooling-off periods for politicians transitioning to the private sector would help curb the influence of lobbyists.

The fight for campaign finance and lobbying reform isn't just a policy issue—it's a moral one. As long as corporations are allowed to buy influence, the interests of the American people will take a back seat to the desires of the wealthy elite. Reclaiming democracy means ensuring that elections are decided by voters, not by corporate donors writing the biggest checks.

Taxing Corporations

Corporate America has been getting away with robbery for decades. While workers pay their taxes, billion-dollar corporations have found countless ways to avoid paying their fair share, exploiting loopholes, offshore tax havens, and friendly politicians willing to slash corporate tax rates. The result is an economic system that shifts the tax burden away from the wealthy and onto working- and middle-class Americans, while the richest companies hoard record profits.

In 2017, the **Tax Cuts and Jobs Act**—championed by President Donald Trump—slashed the corporate tax rate from 35% to 21%. The result was a windfall for corporations, which used the extra cash not to invest in workers or innovation, but to buy back stock, enriching shareholders and executives. Meanwhile, ordinary Americans saw little benefit from the tax cuts, as wages remained stagnant, healthcare costs continued to rise, and income inequality worsened.

This isn't just an American problem—it's a global one. Corporations like **Apple**, **Amazon**, and **Google** have been notorious for using offshore tax havens to shelter their profits and avoid paying taxes. According to a 2020 report from the **Institute on Taxation and Economic Policy**, 55 of the largest U.S. companies paid zero dollars in federal income taxes on $40.5 billion in profits. Some, like Amazon, even received refunds despite posting record earnings. This is not a quirk of the system—it is the system, designed to benefit the ultra-wealthy at the expense of everyone else.

To counter this, we need **tax reform** that forces corporations to pay their fair share. First and foremost, we must raise the corporate tax rate back to pre-2017 levels—or higher. Corporations should not be allowed to profit off of the country's resources, infrastructure, and labor while contributing next to nothing in return. Closing the tax loopholes that allow companies to shelter profits offshore is another key reform. By implementing global minimum tax rates, we can prevent corporations from playing countries against each other in a race to the bottom for tax incentives.

We also need to reintroduce taxes on corporate stock buybacks, which allow corporations to inflate their stock prices and enrich shareholders at the expense of workers and long-term investments. A **financial transaction tax** on stock trades would also curb speculation and ensure that Wall Street contributes to the public good rather than simply enriching itself.

Corporate tax reform would not only generate revenue for desperately needed public services like healthcare, education, and infrastructure—it would also strike at the heart of corporate power. By making corporations pay their fair share, we can begin to chip away at the economic inequality that has concentrated wealth and power in the hands of the few.

Workers' Rights

Corporate control over government has resulted in a systematic erosion of workers' rights over the last few decades. From the rise of the gig economy to the spread of **"right-to-work" laws**, workers across the country have seen their protections dismantled and their bargaining power diminished. To truly disrupt corporate power, we must rebuild and strengthen workers' rights, ensuring that every American has access to fair wages, safe working conditions, and the right to unionize.

One of the most crucial reforms is the passage of the **Protecting the Right to Organize (PRO) Act**, which would be the most significant expansion of labor rights in decades. The PRO Act would make it easier for workers to unionize, ban employer interference in union elections, and prevent companies from retaliating against workers who organize. It would also eliminate **"right-to-work" laws**, which have severely weakened unions by allowing workers to opt out of paying union dues while still benefiting from union-negotiated contracts. These laws, championed by corporate lobbyists, have decimated unions in many states, leaving workers with fewer protections and lower wages.

We must also address the rise of **gig work** and **independent contracting**, which has allowed corporations to evade labor laws by classifying workers as contractors rather than employees. Companies like **Uber** and **DoorDash** have built entire business models on the exploitation of gig workers, denying them healthcare, paid leave, and other benefits while underpaying them and overworking them. The PRO Act would also reclassify many of these workers as employees, granting them the protections and benefits they deserve.

Paid family leave, guaranteed sick days, and a living wage must be non-negotiable aspects of labor policy. For too long, corporations have relied on an exhausted, overworked, and underpaid workforce. The COVID-19 pandemic exposed just how vulnerable workers are in this system, with millions of Americans forced to choose between their health and their paycheck. By strengthening labor protections, we can ensure that no one has to make that choice again.

Reforming labor laws isn't just about improving conditions for workers—it's about shifting the balance of power. When workers have the right to organize and fight for their interests, they can push back against corporate exploitation, forcing companies to prioritize people over profits. Strong labor protections are a critical check on corporate power, and they are essential for building an economy that works for everyone.

Ensuring Democracy Works for All

No discussion of reclaiming power from corporate control can ignore the issue of **voting rights**. As long as corporations and their political allies are allowed to suppress the vote and disenfranchise marginalized communities, our democracy will remain broken. Voting rights are the foundation of democratic power, and without them, every other reform becomes much harder to achieve.

In recent years, there has been a nationwide assault on voting rights, particularly in Republican-controlled states where corporate-backed politicians have enacted laws designed to make it harder for people—especially Black, Latino, and low-income voters—to cast their ballots. These efforts include voter ID laws, cuts to early voting, purges of voter rolls, and the closing of polling places in minority communities. These measures are designed to suppress turnout, ensuring that corporate interests and their political allies maintain control.

To fight back, we must pass comprehensive **voting rights legislation** that expands access to the ballot box, protects against voter suppression, and ensures that every vote is counted. The **For the People Act**, a sweeping reform bill that was introduced in Congress, would address many of these issues by banning partisan gerrymandering, restoring the Voting Rights Act, and implementing automatic voter registration.

In addition to protecting the right to vote, we must also ensure that elections are fair and secure. The rise of voter disenfranchisement through disinformation campaigns and tactics that disproportionately impact communities of color is part of a larger strategy to weaken the political power of ordinary people. Without protecting the integrity of our elections, corporate interests will continue to dominate the political process.

Voting rights reform is about more than just protecting access to the ballot—it's about ensuring that democracy works for everyone, not just the wealthy elite. When more people vote, we can elect leaders who are accountable to the people, not to corporate donors.

Collective Action

While policy reforms are critical, they won't happen without collective action. Corporate power has become so entrenched that it will take mass mobilization, protests, strikes, and sustained political pressure to push through meaningful change. The victories of the past—whether they were the **New Deal**, the **Civil Rights Movement**, or the fight for women's suffrage—were won through collective action, not through polite lobbying or negotiations behind closed doors.

We need a new era of mass movements, where ordinary people organize to demand justice, equality, and an end to corporate domination. This means supporting labor strikes, joining protests against environmental destruction, and holding corporations accountable for their abuses. It means building coalitions across race, class, gender, and geography, recognizing that the fight for justice is a fight that must be waged on many fronts.

Movements like the **Fight for $15**, **Black Lives Matter**, and the **Sunrise Movement** have already shown that collective action works. These movements have forced corporations and politicians to confront uncomfortable truths, and they have built the kind of pressure that leads to real change. But we need more than sporadic movements—we need sustained organizing that keeps the pressure on, year after year.

Reclaiming power from corporate America won't be easy, and it won't happen overnight. But through a combination of bold policy reforms, voting rights protections, and collective action, we can begin to dismantle the corporate stranglehold on our government, economy, and society. This is a fight for the soul of our democracy, and it's a fight we must win.

The Weaponization of Economic Despair

The End of Secure Employment

In the post-World War II era, America's economy was built on the promise of stable, secure employment. Millions of Americans could rely on full-time jobs with decent wages, healthcare, pensions, and other benefits. This was the foundation of the American middle class, a period often referred to as the **Golden Age of Capitalism**, where unions were strong, labor had power, and corporations were expected to provide for their employees.

But this era didn't last. Starting in the 1970s, a shift began—a deliberate move by corporations to increase profits by reducing labor costs. Secure, full-time jobs with benefits were slowly replaced with precarious work. The rise of **outsourcing**, **offshoring**, **temporary work**, and **part-time employment** became the new norm. These changes were not just about adapting to new economic conditions; they were about shifting the balance of power away from workers and back to corporations.

One of the most insidious strategies used to weaken labor was the rise of **independent contracting** and **gig work**. Gig work, hailed as a new frontier of labor freedom, has been anything but liberating for the millions of workers who now find themselves working without healthcare, retirement benefits, or job security. Corporations like **Uber**, **Lyft**, and **DoorDash** have perfected the art of selling precarity as empowerment, convincing workers that they are "entrepreneurs" when, in reality, they are just as dependent on their corporate overlords as any full-time employee. The only difference is, now these workers bear all the risk.

Gig workers aren't alone. The rise of part-time and temporary jobs has spread across virtually every industry. From retail workers to teachers to healthcare professionals, millions of Americans now find themselves working jobs where they can't rely on a stable schedule, where hours are cut on a whim, and where benefits are a distant dream. This shift has allowed corporations to save billions in labor costs while leaving workers in a state of perpetual insecurity.

The Illusion of Job Flexibility

The corporate push to normalize precarious work has been cloaked in the language of "flexibility." Companies like Uber and other gig economy giants argue that gig work gives workers the freedom to choose their hours, be their own bosses, and work on their own terms. But scratch the surface, and it becomes clear that this flexibility is a trap. Gig workers may have the flexibility to log in and out of an app, but they have no control over the algorithm that determines their pay, the availability of jobs, or their ability to make a living.

This illusion of freedom is part of a larger strategy to disguise exploitation as opportunity. Gig workers don't get health insurance, paid sick leave, or unemployment benefits. They don't receive any of the protections afforded to full-time employees because they are classified as "independent contractors," a legal loophole that corporations have exploited to avoid providing basic benefits. Meanwhile, workers are forced to shoulder the costs of doing business—whether it's paying for gas, vehicle maintenance, or the wear and tear on their bodies—while the corporations that control these platforms rake in billions.

The rise of gig work is a direct result of corporate America's refusal to invest in its workforce. Rather than provide stable jobs with decent benefits, corporations have embraced a business model that leaves workers vulnerable and expendable. This is no accident—it's a deliberate attempt to maintain control over a workforce that has no power to organize, no bargaining power, and no safety net to fall back on.

The Fear of Unemployment

The corporate shift toward precarious work isn't just about saving money—it's about creating fear. The fear of unemployment is one of the most powerful tools corporations have to keep workers compliant and desperate. When workers know that they can be replaced at any moment, when they live in constant fear of losing their jobs, they are far less likely to demand higher wages, better working conditions, or the right to unionize.

This fear is heightened by the fact that in today's economy, finding a new job is no longer a guarantee of stability. Unemployment has become a looming specter for millions of workers, and the consequences of losing a job can be catastrophic. In an economy where healthcare is tied to employment, where wages have stagnated for decades, and where affordable housing is increasingly out of reach, losing a job means losing everything.

Corporations know this, and they exploit it. By keeping workers in a state of constant insecurity, they ensure that their workforce remains docile, compliant, and unwilling to rock the boat. The threat of unemployment is enough to keep workers in line, even as wages stagnate, benefits disappear, and working conditions deteriorate. And with **automation** and **outsourcing** looming over many industries, workers are acutely aware that their jobs could be replaced by machines or cheaper labor overseas at any moment.

Stagnant Wages and Rising Costs

For decades, wages for American workers have remained stagnant, even as corporate profits have soared to record levels.

While the cost of living has continued to rise—housing, healthcare, education, and childcare all becoming more expensive—workers have seen little to no increase in their paychecks. This wage stagnation is a direct result of corporate America's decision to prioritize shareholder profits over the well-being of its workforce.

In the post-World War II period, wages and productivity grew together. As workers became more productive, their wages increased, and the middle class thrived. But starting in the 1970s, that link was severed. Productivity continued to rise, but wages stagnated, while corporate profits skyrocketed. The gap between worker pay and CEO compensation has grown to staggering levels, with the average CEO earning **320 times** what the average worker makes. This is not an accident—it is the result of deliberate corporate policies designed to extract as much wealth as possible from workers while giving back as little as possible.

At the same time, the cost of living has skyrocketed. Housing prices have surged, healthcare costs have become unmanageable, and the price of education has spiraled out of control, leaving millions of Americans drowning in debt. The average worker is now forced to take on multiple jobs, work longer hours, and make impossible choices between paying for rent, healthcare, and basic necessities.

This is no accident. Corporate America has engineered an economy that forces workers to accept less, even as the cost of living continues to rise. And with wages stuck in place, millions of Americans are falling further behind, trapped in a cycle of poverty and debt from which there is no escape. For corporations, this economic despair is not a bug—it's a feature. A desperate workforce is a compliant workforce, and as long as workers are struggling to survive, they won't have the time, energy, or resources to fight back.

The Destruction of the Social Safety Net

One of the most devastating aspects of corporate America's war on workers has been the systematic dismantling of the social safety net. Programs like **unemployment insurance**, **Medicaid**, **food assistance**, and **housing subsidies** have been slashed, underfunded, or subjected to endless bureaucratic red tape, leaving millions of Americans without the safety nets they need to survive.

The destruction of the social safety net is a deliberate strategy by corporations and their political allies to keep workers vulnerable and dependent on low-wage jobs. Without access to healthcare, unemployment benefits, or affordable housing, workers have no choice but to accept whatever job is available, no matter how exploitative. The fear of poverty, homelessness, and illness keeps workers in line, forcing them to stay in jobs that offer no benefits, no security, and no future.

For example, the **Temporary Assistance for Needy Families (TANF)** program, once a vital lifeline for low-income families, has been gutted over the years, leaving millions of people with no safety net to fall back on. The **Supplemental Nutrition Assistance Program (SNAP)**, commonly known as food stamps, has also been targeted for cuts, despite being one of the most effective anti-poverty programs in the country. These programs, which were designed to help people during tough times, have been slashed to the bone, leaving millions of Americans on the brink of disaster.

Corporations have long pushed the narrative that government assistance creates "dependency," and they have used this myth to justify the destruction of social welfare programs. But the truth is that these programs are essential for maintaining a decent standard of living for millions of people who have been left behind by the corporate-driven economy. By dismantling the safety net, corporations ensure that workers remain desperate, fearful, and unable to fight back.

Economic Despair as a Weapon

Economic despair isn't just a byproduct of the corporate takeover—it's a weapon, wielded by corporations to keep workers too exhausted, too scared, and too beaten down to resist. Fear of unemployment, fear of poverty, fear of losing healthcare or housing—these are the tools that corporate America uses to maintain control over the workforce. When people are desperate, they will accept anything, and corporations know it.

The system is designed to keep workers in a perpetual state of insecurity. Whether it's through precarious employment, stagnant wages, or the destruction of social safety nets, corporate America has ensured that millions of Americans are too busy surviving to organize, protest, or demand their fair share of the wealth they create. This is economic control on a massive scale, and it has been devastatingly effective.

The corporate weaponization of economic despair has led to a society where millions of people live paycheck to paycheck, where the fear of job loss is a constant presence, and where workers are afraid to demand better wages or conditions because they know how easily they can be replaced. This fear is corrosive—it erodes solidarity, weakens collective action, and keeps workers divided and isolated. And as long as corporations can maintain this fear, they can maintain their control.

The Engineered Crisis of Economic Despair

The creation of a desperate workforce is not an accident—it is a deliberate, calculated strategy designed to maximize profits and maintain corporate power. By stripping workers of secure employment, pushing them into precarious jobs, and dismantling the social safety nets that once provided a buffer against economic disaster, corporations have created a system where economic despair is the norm.

This despair is not just a byproduct of corporate greed—it is a weapon, used to keep workers compliant, divided, and too fearful to fight back. As long as workers are struggling to survive, as long as they are fearful of losing their jobs, their homes, and their healthcare, corporations will continue to exploit them, extracting as much wealth as possible while giving back as little as they can get away with.

Manufactured Poverty

Poverty in America is not an inevitable consequence of a complex economy—it is a manufactured crisis, created and sustained by corporate policies designed to suppress wages, exploit labor, and keep people dependent on low-paying jobs. The United States, one of the wealthiest nations in the world, has an appalling rate of poverty, with nearly 38 million people living below the federal poverty line. But poverty isn't just about a lack of money—it's about the systemic barriers that keep people trapped in a cycle of economic despair.

The roots of poverty in America can be traced directly to the corporate assault on wages and workers' rights. For decades, corporations have fought tooth and nail to suppress wage growth, undermining efforts to raise the minimum wage, gutting labor protections, and outsourcing jobs to countries where labor is cheaper and regulations are weak. The result has been stagnant wages for American workers, even as the cost of living continues to rise. The federal minimum wage has remained at a paltry **$7.25** per hour since 2009, a figure that is completely out of touch with the realities of today's economy.

For millions of Americans, working a full-time job is no longer enough to lift them out of poverty. The **Fight for $15**, a movement advocating for a living wage, has highlighted the plight of fast food, retail, and other low-wage workers who are forced to rely on public assistance to survive. Corporations like **McDonald's** and **Walmart**, which post billions in profits each year, pay their workers poverty wages, while their executives take home millions in bonuses and stock options. These companies have perfected the art of corporate welfare, forcing the government—and, by extension, the taxpayer—to subsidize their workforce through food stamps, Medicaid, and housing assistance, all while avoiding any responsibility for providing a living wage.

Beyond wage suppression, corporations have also ensured that poverty is passed down from generation to generation. Low-income families face systemic barriers to education, healthcare, and housing that keep them trapped in poverty. The **school-to-prison pipeline**, underfunded public schools, and the lack of affordable childcare make it nearly impossible for poor families to break the cycle. Corporations, meanwhile, lobby against any meaningful reforms to these systems, knowing full well that an educated and empowered workforce would demand better wages and working conditions.

The criminalization of poverty is another weapon in the corporate arsenal. **Wage theft**, where employers steal money that rightfully belongs to their employees by withholding overtime pay, forcing workers to work off the clock, or refusing to pay minimum wage, is rampant across industries. It is estimated that U.S. workers lose **$50 billion** annually to wage theft—more than the combined total of robberies, burglaries, and car thefts. Yet wage theft is rarely prosecuted, and companies that engage in these practices often face little more than a slap on the wrist. For corporations, wage theft is simply another way to maximize profits, with the added benefit of keeping workers poor and powerless.

Debt as a Tool of Control

If poverty is the weapon, debt is the chains that bind. Over the last few decades, debt has become a central tool of corporate control, with millions of Americans now shackled by crushing levels of personal debt. Whether it's credit card debt, student loans, medical debt, or payday loans, corporations have found countless ways to exploit financial desperation and turn debt into a profit center. And for the millions of Americans drowning in debt, the effects are devastating, trapping them in a cycle of financial insecurity and limiting their ability to improve their lives.

One of the most insidious forms of debt is **student loan debt**, which now totals over **$1.7 trillion** in the United States. What was once seen as an investment in the future—pursuing higher education to improve one's economic prospects—has become a financial nightmare for millions of Americans. As public funding for universities has been slashed and the cost of tuition has skyrocketed, students have been forced to take out massive loans to pay for their education. Corporations like **Sallie Mae** and **Navient**, which service and profit from student loans, have turned education into a business, preying on students who have no choice but to borrow.

For many graduates, the reality is grim: they leave school with tens of thousands of dollars in debt and enter a job market that offers low wages and few benefits. Unable to keep up with payments, many find themselves trapped in a cycle of debt, unable to buy a home, start a family, or save for the future. The student debt crisis has effectively robbed an entire generation of financial stability, all while lining the pockets of corporate lenders and debt collectors.

But student debt is just one piece of the puzzle. **Medical debt** is another massive burden for millions of Americans, a result of a broken healthcare system that puts profits over people. Even with insurance, many Americans face exorbitant out-of-pocket costs for basic medical care. A single illness, accident, or surgery can plunge a family into financial ruin, forcing them to take on debt just to stay alive. Hospitals and healthcare providers, many of which operate as for-profit corporations, routinely send unpaid medical bills to collection agencies, leaving patients with ruined credit and no hope of ever paying off their debts.

And then there's **payday loans**, the most predatory form of lending that preys on the desperate. Payday loan companies, which operate with little regulation in many states, target low-income individuals who are in urgent need of cash, offering short-term loans at exorbitant interest rates—sometimes as high as **400%**. These loans are designed to trap borrowers in a cycle of debt, as they often cannot pay back the loan in full and are forced to take out additional loans just to cover the interest. Corporations in the payday loan industry rake in billions each year by exploiting the financial desperation of the poorest Americans.

Debt is not just a financial burden—it's a tool of control. When people are weighed down by debt, they are less likely to take risks, less likely to demand better wages, and less likely to fight back against the system that has trapped them. Corporations know this, and they use debt to keep workers in a constant state of fear and insecurity. A workforce that is drowning in debt is a workforce that will accept low wages, poor working conditions, and endless exploitation.

The Explosion of Inequality

At the heart of the weaponization of economic despair is the explosion of inequality that has defined the American economy over the past several decades. Corporate America has created a system where the rich get richer, and everyone else is left to fight over the scraps. The concentration of wealth in the hands of a tiny elite, while millions struggle to survive, is not just an unfortunate outcome of capitalism—it is a deliberate design, crafted by corporations and their political allies to ensure that power remains firmly in the hands of the few.

The numbers speak for themselves. The top **1%** of Americans now control more wealth than the bottom **90%** combined. Corporate executives take home record-breaking salaries and bonuses, while workers see their wages stagnate or decline. The **CEO-to-worker pay ratio** has ballooned to **320 to 1**, with some CEOs making more in a day than their employees make in a year. This grotesque inequality is not just immoral—it is unsustainable.

How did we get here? The answer lies in the corporate takeover of government policy. Starting in the **1980s**, under the guise of **Reaganomics** and **trickle-down economics**, corporations successfully lobbied for tax cuts for the wealthy, deregulation of industries, and the dismantling of social safety nets. The result was a massive transfer of wealth from the middle and working classes to the richest Americans. Corporate tax rates have been slashed, while workers are taxed on every dollar they earn. Financial regulations that once kept Wall Street in check have been rolled back, allowing corporations to engage in risky speculation and reap huge rewards while leaving the rest of the country to deal with the fallout.

At the same time, the **rise of monopolies** has further concentrated wealth and power in the hands of a few mega-corporations. Companies like **Amazon**, **Facebook**, and **Google** dominate their industries, crushing competition and amassing staggering fortunes. These corporations have the resources to lobby for favorable policies, avoid taxes, and squash any attempts at meaningful regulation. The result is an economy where a handful of companies control vast swaths of the market, leaving small businesses, workers, and consumers with little power to push back.

Inequality isn't just about money—it's about power. The more wealth corporations and the ultra-rich accumulate, the more influence they wield over our political system, our economy, and our society. This concentration of power allows them to shape laws, regulations, and policies to benefit themselves, ensuring that the gap between the rich and the rest of us continues to grow.

The Human Cost of Inequality

The economic inequality engineered by corporate America has devastating consequences for the health and well-being of ordinary Americans. Inequality affects every aspect of life, from health outcomes to educational opportunities to housing stability. Those at the top of the economic ladder enjoy better healthcare, longer lives, and more opportunities, while those at the bottom are left to struggle with the physical, mental, and emotional toll of poverty.

Health disparities are one of the most glaring consequences of inequality. Wealthy Americans can afford the best healthcare money can buy, while low-income individuals are forced to rely on an underfunded and inaccessible healthcare system. The **life expectancy gap** between the richest and poorest Americans has widened dramatically in recent years, with wealthy individuals living up to **15 years longer** than their poorer counterparts. This disparity is fueled by unequal access to healthcare, as well as the stresses of poverty, which lead to higher rates of chronic illness, mental health issues, and substance abuse.

Housing inequality is another major consequence of the economic system created by corporate America. As housing prices continue to rise, millions of Americans are struggling to afford a place to live. **Rent** has skyrocketed in cities across the country, and homeownership is increasingly out of reach for younger generations. At the same time, the rise of corporate landlords has turned housing into a speculative investment, with companies buying up properties, driving up prices, and leaving ordinary people with fewer and fewer options.

The result of this housing crisis is a growing homelessness epidemic. More than **half a million Americans** are homeless on any given night, a figure that has been steadily rising in recent years. In cities like **Los Angeles**, **San Francisco**, and **New York**, homelessness has reached crisis levels, with tent cities and encampments becoming a common sight. Meanwhile, corporate landlords continue to profit from rising rents and evictions, with little concern for the human cost.

The human toll of inequality is staggering. From poverty to debt to homelessness, millions of Americans are trapped in a system that values profit over people. Corporate America has engineered an economy where the rich are insulated from the consequences of their greed, while the rest of us are left to suffer the consequences.

Inequality Is the Weapon

Inequality is not just a symptom of a broken system—it is the system. Corporate America has weaponized economic despair, using poverty, debt, and inequality to maintain control over society. The more unequal our economy becomes, the more power corporations and the wealthy elite hold over the rest of us.

Campaign Finance

One of the most obvious and egregious ways that corporate America has cemented its control over politics is through **campaign finance**. The influence of money in politics has reached unprecedented levels, with corporations and wealthy individuals pouring billions of dollars into elections to secure the loyalty of lawmakers. The result is a political class that is more beholden to corporate donors than to the people they are supposed to represent.

The turning point in this process came with the **Citizens United v. FEC** decision in 2010, when the Supreme Court ruled that corporations and other organizations could spend unlimited amounts of money on elections, as long as the spending was independent of the candidates' campaigns. This decision unleashed a flood of corporate money into the political system, giving rise to **Super PACs** (Political Action Committees) and **dark money** groups that could spend without disclosing their donors. What followed was the transformation of American democracy into a marketplace, where political influence is for sale to the highest bidder.

The consequences of this corporate takeover of campaign finance have been profound. Corporations now wield enormous influence over which candidates run for office, which policies are prioritized, and which laws are passed. Candidates who refuse to toe the corporate line are starved of campaign funds, while those who promise to advance corporate interests are showered with donations. This dynamic has created a political system where lawmakers are more concerned with appeasing their corporate backers than with addressing the needs of their constituents.

Take, for example, the fossil fuel industry, which has spent billions lobbying against climate change legislation and funding the campaigns of politicians who deny the science of global warming. Or the pharmaceutical industry, which has used its vast financial resources to prevent any meaningful reform of the healthcare system, ensuring that drug prices remain sky-high while millions of Americans go without necessary medications. In both cases, corporate money has distorted the political process, making it nearly impossible for lawmakers to pass laws that protect the public interest.

Moreover, the dominance of corporate money in politics has created a revolving door between government and the private sector. Politicians, regulators, and government officials who leave public office often go on to take high-paying jobs as corporate lobbyists, using their insider knowledge and connections to further corporate agendas. This revolving door ensures that corporate interests are always represented in the halls of power, while the concerns of ordinary citizens are marginalized.

Lobbying

While campaign finance has given corporations a direct line to lawmakers, **lobbying** is the mechanism through which corporate influence is most effectively wielded. Lobbying is, in essence, a form of legalized corruption, where corporations hire well-connected professionals—often former politicians or government officials—to advocate on their behalf and influence legislation, regulations, and public policy.

The lobbying industry is vast and immensely powerful. In 2022 alone, over **$3.7 billion** was spent on lobbying in Washington, with the vast majority of that money coming from corporations and industry groups. The industries that spend the most on lobbying—healthcare, finance, energy, and technology—are the ones that benefit the most from favorable policies, regulations, and tax breaks. These industries have built entire networks of lobbyists whose sole job is to protect corporate profits, no matter the cost to the public.

The **pharmaceutical industry**, for example, has spent billions of dollars over the years to ensure that no meaningful reforms to drug pricing laws are enacted. Lobbyists for companies like **Pfizer, Johnson & Johnson**, and **Merck** routinely descend on Capitol Hill to pressure lawmakers into maintaining the status quo, where drug companies can charge whatever they want for life-saving medications. Meanwhile, Americans pay the highest drug prices in the world, with little recourse to challenge the industry's stranglehold on healthcare policy.

Similarly, the **financial industry** has used its lobbying power to block regulations designed to prevent another economic meltdown like the 2008 financial crisis. Banks and investment firms, including giants like **Goldman Sachs** and **JPMorgan Chase**, have spent billions lobbying against consumer protections and financial regulations, ensuring that Wall Street can continue to engage in risky, profit-driven behavior without facing significant consequences.

Lobbying isn't just about protecting corporate profits—it's about shaping the entire framework of public policy to reflect corporate interests. From environmental regulations to labor laws to trade agreements, corporate lobbyists work behind the scenes to ensure that laws are written in ways that benefit the bottom line. These lobbyists often draft legislation themselves, presenting it to lawmakers as "model bills" that are ready to be passed with minimal debate. The result is a political system where corporations, not citizens, write the laws that govern our society.

Voter Suppression

As corporate power in politics has grown, so too has the effort to suppress the voices of ordinary citizens—particularly those who are most likely to oppose corporate interests. **Voter suppression** has become a key strategy in maintaining corporate dominance, as politicians backed by corporate money seek to limit the political participation of marginalized communities, working-class voters, and people of color.

Voter suppression takes many forms, from restrictive voter ID laws to gerrymandering to the closure of polling places in predominantly minority neighborhoods. These tactics are designed to make it harder for certain groups of people to vote, thus ensuring that the electorate remains skewed in favor of corporate-backed candidates and policies.

One of the most blatant examples of voter suppression occurred in **Georgia** during the 2018 gubernatorial election, where **Brian Kemp**, the Republican candidate who was also the state's top election official, oversaw a massive voter purge that disproportionately affected Black voters. Kemp's office purged **1.4 million** voters from the rolls between 2012 and 2018, citing dubious claims of voter fraud. Despite widespread outcry, Kemp won the election by a narrow margin, ensuring that the state would continue to be governed by politicians aligned with corporate interests.

In **Texas**, one of the most gerrymandered states in the country, voter suppression is rampant. The state's Republican-controlled legislature has passed a series of laws designed to make it harder for people to vote, including strict voter ID requirements, limitations on early voting, and the closure of polling places in minority-heavy areas. These efforts have disproportionately affected communities of color and low-income voters, who are less likely to have the necessary identification or the ability to travel long distances to vote. By suppressing these votes, corporate-backed politicians in Texas have been able to maintain control over state government, passing laws that favor corporations over workers, consumers, and the environment.

The suppression of voting rights is not an isolated phenomenon—it is part of a larger strategy to entrench corporate power and weaken democracy. By making it harder for people to vote, corporations and their political allies can ensure that the electorate remains skewed in their favor, allowing them to pass laws that benefit the wealthy elite while ignoring the needs of the broader population.

A Rigged System

The concentration of corporate power in politics represents a profound threat to democracy itself. When corporations control elections, write laws, and suppress votes, the very idea of democratic governance is called into question. The result is an oligarchy, where the wealthy few dictate the rules of society, and the vast majority of people are left with little power to influence the course of their own lives.

This is not just a crisis of governance—it is a crisis of legitimacy. When people feel that their votes don't matter, when they see politicians who are more responsive to corporate donors than to their constituents, they lose faith in the system. Voter turnout declines, political engagement diminishes, and the public becomes increasingly cynical about the possibility of meaningful change.

But corporate America doesn't fear this cynicism—in fact, it benefits from it. A disengaged and disillusioned electorate is easier to manipulate, easier to control. As long as people believe that the system is rigged and that their voices don't matter, corporations can continue to operate with impunity, amassing wealth and power while the rest of the country falls further into despair.

The threat to democracy is not abstract—it is real, and it is urgent. Corporate control of politics has already led to a system where inequality is rampant, where workers are exploited, and where the environment is sacrificed for profit. If left unchecked, this concentration of power will only deepen, leading to a future where democracy exists in name only, and where the interests of the many are permanently subordinated to the interests of the few.

Fighting for Democracy, Fighting for Justice

The weaponization of economic despair is not just about poverty or inequality—it's about power. Corporate America has used its vast wealth to corrupt the political system, ensuring that laws and policies are written to benefit the wealthy elite while the rest of the country struggles to get by. This concentration of political power in the hands of corporations represents the greatest threat to democracy in our time, and if we are to reclaim our future, we must confront it head-on.

Neo-Feudalism and the Corporate Lords

The Rise of the Corporate Lords

The parallels between medieval feudalism and today's corporate-dominated society are more than just metaphorical. Under the old feudal system, the lords owned the land, controlled the means of production, and held absolute power over the peasants who worked the land in exchange for protection and survival. Today, the land has been replaced by capital, and the lords by corporate executives, CEOs, and billionaires who control the means of production—factories, warehouses, data centers, and the financial institutions that shape our economy. Meanwhile, ordinary workers are the modern equivalent of serfs, tied to their jobs not by chains or contracts but by debt, low wages, and the constant threat of unemployment.

In medieval times, the nobility ruled over vast estates, collecting rent from peasants and extracting labor from those who worked the land. Today, the corporate elite extract their wealth in much the same way—by controlling capital, intellectual property, and resources that the rest of society depends on. Companies like **Amazon**, **Google**, and **Facebook** don't just dominate their industries; they control entire sectors of the economy, collecting rents in the form of profits from nearly every aspect of modern life.

The new corporate lords—CEOs like **Jeff Bezos, Mark Zuckerberg**, and **Elon Musk**—are not simply wealthy businessmen; they are the de facto rulers of the economy. Their companies dominate the marketplace to such an extent that they have created monopolies or near-monopolies, which allow them to set the rules for entire industries, from online retail to social media to space exploration. These corporate titans are worth more than many small nations, and they wield their wealth like political power, influencing governments, buying elections, and shaping public policy to serve their own interests.

The concentration of wealth in the hands of these corporate lords is staggering. As of 2021, the world's richest 1% held more wealth than the entire bottom half of the global population. In the United States, the wealthiest 10% own nearly 90% of all stocks, bonds, and mutual funds, leaving the rest of the population with little financial security or power. Meanwhile, CEO pay has skyrocketed, with the average CEO earning over **300 times** what the average worker makes. This isn't just a matter of inequality—it's a new form of economic feudalism, where the few hold all the power and the many are left to struggle for survival.

These modern lords don't rule through military force or legal decrees, as medieval lords did; they rule through economic coercion. Workers are kept in line not by physical chains but by the need to pay rent, buy food, and keep the lights on. The threat of losing a job, losing health insurance, or falling behind on bills is enough to ensure that most people will accept whatever terms their corporate overlords impose. In this system, the rich grow richer by extracting wealth from workers who are left with little more than survival wages.

Serfdom in the Modern Age

In medieval times, serfs were tied to the land, forced to work for their lords in exchange for protection and a place to live. Today's workers are tied to their jobs through **wage slavery** and **debt**, trapped in an economic system where the cost of living continues to rise while wages remain stagnant. The result is a workforce that is increasingly dependent on low-paying, precarious jobs, with little hope of escaping the cycle of economic insecurity.

The concept of **wage slavery** refers to the idea that workers, especially those in low-wage jobs, are forced to sell their labor under conditions that leave them with little autonomy or control over their lives. In today's gig economy, workers for companies like **Uber, Lyft,** and **Instacart** are often classified as "independent contractors," a designation that strips them of basic labor protections like health insurance, paid leave, and the right to unionize. These workers are told they have "flexibility" and "freedom," but in reality, they are at the mercy of corporate algorithms that determine when, where, and how much they can work.

For millions of Americans, wage slavery is compounded by **debt**, which acts as a modern-day form of serfdom. In medieval times, serfs were indebted to their lords, paying rent or taxes in exchange for protection. Today, debt is used as a tool of control by corporations, banks, and financial institutions. **Student debt, credit card debt, medical debt,** and **payday loans** are all mechanisms that trap people in cycles of poverty and dependency. With the cost of living far outpacing wage growth, many workers are forced to take on debt just to make ends meet, leaving them with little room to save, invest, or improve their financial situation.

The total student debt in the U.S. has surpassed **$1.7 trillion**, with millions of Americans trapped in a system where they are forced to pay off loans for decades, often without any realistic hope of financial independence. This debt effectively ties people to their jobs, as they cannot afford to take time off, change careers, or pursue entrepreneurial ventures. They are modern-day serfs, bound to the corporate system not by legal contracts but by the financial chains of debt.

Rentier Capitalism: Extracting Wealth from the Many

One of the defining features of neo-feudalism is the rise of **rentier capitalism**, a system where the wealthy elite extract wealth not by producing goods or services but by controlling assets—

property, intellectual property, and capital—that the rest of society must pay to use. In this system, the corporate lords do not need to work or innovate; they simply need to own the right assets and collect rent from those who do.

In today's economy, rentier capitalism manifests in many forms. **Landlords** and **real estate developers** extract wealth from renters by driving up housing costs and limiting the supply of affordable housing. In cities like **San Francisco**, **New York**, and **Los Angeles**, the housing market has become so inflated that millions of people are priced out of homeownership and forced to pay exorbitant rents to corporate landlords who own vast swaths of the housing market. These landlords, many of whom are hedge funds or private equity firms, view housing not as a human right but as a commodity to be traded and exploited for profit.

Intellectual property is another area where corporate lords have established monopolies, extracting wealth from the rest of society. Companies like **Google**, **Apple**, and **Amazon** control vast amounts of data, patents, and proprietary technology that the rest of the world relies on. These companies have built empires by controlling access to the tools and platforms that are essential for modern life. Whether it's the **App Store**, **Google Search**, or **Amazon Web Services**, the corporate lords of Silicon Valley extract wealth by controlling the infrastructure of the digital age.

Meanwhile, the **financialization** of the economy has turned everything from education to healthcare to housing into opportunities for speculation and profit. **Private equity firms** and **hedge funds** have become the new feudal lords of Wall Street, buying up companies, stripping them of assets, and leaving workers to pick up the pieces. This is the essence of rentier capitalism—wealth is extracted not by creating value but by siphoning off the wealth of others.

Rentier capitalism is a direct assault on the working class, as it shifts wealth upward while providing little in return. Workers who cannot afford to buy a home, start a business, or invest in their future are left to pay rent—whether it's for housing, for access to data, or for the basic necessities of life—to the corporate lords who control the economy.

Corporate Control of Land and Resources

In the medieval feudal system, control of land was the foundation of wealth and power. Today, land and resources remain central to the power of the corporate lords, who control everything from agricultural production to the energy that powers our homes and businesses. Corporations like **Monsanto**, **ExxonMobil**, and **Nestlé** have monopolized the resources that the rest of society relies on, using their control over land, water, and energy to extract wealth from consumers and maintain their dominance.

The corporate control of land has reached new heights with the rise of **agribusiness** giants like **Monsanto** and **Bayer**, which have transformed farming into an industrial operation where small farmers are squeezed out of the market, and agricultural workers are subjected to low wages and brutal working conditions. These corporations control the supply chains for food, seeds, and livestock, leaving small farmers and rural communities at their mercy. In many cases, small farmers are forced to lease land or buy seeds from these giant agribusinesses, turning them into modern-day serfs who work the land for the benefit of the corporate lords.

Similarly, **Big Oil** companies like **ExxonMobil**, **Chevron**, and **BP** dominate the energy sector, controlling the extraction, production, and distribution of the resources that power the global economy. These corporations hold immense political and economic power, and their ability to influence governments, block environmental regulations, and suppress renewable energy alternatives has cemented their position as the lords of modern energy production.

Water, one of the most basic human necessities, has also been transformed into a commodity by corporations like **Nestlé**, which controls vast amounts of freshwater resources around the world. In regions facing water scarcity, private corporations have monopolized access to water, selling it back to consumers at a premium while leaving local communities with little say in how their resources are managed.

The Modern Feudal Lords

The rise of neo-feudalism in the corporate era has created a system where a small group of corporate lords hold all the power, wealth, and resources, while the rest of society is left to toil under increasingly precarious conditions. The parallels between today's corporate overlords and the feudal lords of medieval times are striking—both systems are built on the exploitation of labor, the control of land and resources, and the extraction of wealth from the many to enrich the few.

In this new form of feudalism, workers, renters, and consumers are the modern serfs, trapped in a system where economic mobility is increasingly out of reach, and the corporate elite hold all the cards. The next section will explore how this neo-feudal system has not only deepened economic inequality but also reshaped the very structure of society, creating a new form of class hierarchy that leaves most people powerless in the face of corporate domination.

The Corporate Aristocracy

As corporate America consolidates its power and wealth, a new class system has emerged—one that eerily mirrors the rigid social hierarchies of the medieval feudal era. This corporate class structure creates clear divisions between the elite "lords" of the economy, the dwindling middle class, and an ever-growing underclass of workers who are increasingly locked out of opportunities for advancement. In this new system, mobility is limited, and economic security is reserved for the few at the top, while the rest struggle just to survive.

At the top of the corporate hierarchy sits the **corporate aristocracy**, a class of billionaires, CEOs, and executives who wield immense power over both the economy and politics. These individuals—often hailed as "visionaries" or "geniuses"—enjoy levels of wealth and privilege that would have been unimaginable even a few decades ago. They control the largest corporations, shape the global economy, and use their vast fortunes to influence public policy, elections, and media narratives. In many ways, they have become the modern-day equivalent of the medieval nobility, ruling over vast economic empires while remaining insulated from the challenges faced by ordinary people.

The wealth gap between the corporate aristocracy and the rest of society has reached staggering proportions. In 2021, the wealthiest **1%** of Americans owned more than **40%** of the nation's wealth, while the bottom **50%** held just **2%**. At the very top of the economic ladder are individuals like **Jeff Bezos**, **Elon Musk**, and **Mark Zuckerberg**, whose personal fortunes exceed the GDPs of many small nations. These corporate lords don't just control businesses—they control entire industries, from tech to retail to finance.

The power of the corporate aristocracy extends far beyond the boardroom. Many of these billionaires use their wealth to buy political influence, ensuring that laws and policies are written to protect their interests. Whether through **Super PACs**, direct campaign contributions, or personal relationships with politicians, the corporate elite have effectively bought themselves a seat at the table where decisions are made. This is not democracy—it's oligarchy, where a small group of the wealthy elite holds disproportionate influence over public life.

One of the most disturbing aspects of this new corporate aristocracy is the way it has been normalized and celebrated in

American culture. Billionaires are often portrayed as self-made success stories, lauded for their "entrepreneurial spirit" and "innovation." But this narrative obscures the reality that much of their wealth is built on the exploitation of labor, monopolistic practices, and tax avoidance. The myth of the self-made billionaire serves to justify the extreme inequality that defines this new corporate feudal order, reinforcing the idea that those at the top deserve their wealth, while those at the bottom are responsible for their own poverty.

The Hollowing Out of the Middle Class

In the old feudal system, the middle class barely existed. Society was largely divided between the nobility and the peasants, with little room for upward mobility. Today, the middle class is under siege, as corporate policies and economic trends have systematically hollowed out the economic security that once defined middle-class life. The **American Dream**—the idea that hard work and perseverance could lead to upward mobility and financial stability—is slipping out of reach for millions of people, as wages stagnate, costs rise, and job security disappears.

For decades after World War II, the middle class was the backbone of the American economy. **Unionized jobs**, particularly in manufacturing, provided workers with decent wages, benefits, and the ability to buy homes, send their children to college, and retire with dignity. But starting in the 1970s, the corporate assault on labor—through outsourcing, offshoring, and automation—began to erode these middle-class jobs. Entire industries, from steel manufacturing to textiles, were shipped overseas, leaving millions of American workers unemployed or forced into low-wage service jobs with no benefits or job security.

At the same time, the **gig economy** and **independent contracting** became increasingly normalized, further undermining the security of the middle class. Companies like **Uber**, **Lyft**, and **TaskRabbit** have built their business models on the idea of short-term, freelance work, which offers flexibility but no long-term stability. Many middle-class workers who once enjoyed the security of full-time employment now find themselves cobbling together multiple jobs just to make ends meet, with little hope of ever achieving financial security.

The rise of **student debt** has also played a central role in the decline of the middle class. For many young people, a college degree was once seen as a ticket to upward mobility. But today, higher education has become prohibitively expensive, forcing millions of students to take on massive amounts of debt just to get a degree. With wages stagnant and jobs scarce, many graduates find themselves unable to pay off their loans, leaving them trapped in a cycle of debt that prevents them from achieving the traditional markers of middle-class life, such as buying a home or starting a family.

The erosion of the middle class is not just an economic issue—it's a social one. The middle class has historically been a stabilizing force in American society, serving as a buffer between the wealthy elite and the working poor. As the middle class shrinks, this buffer is disappearing, leaving a society that is increasingly divided between the ultra-wealthy and the economically insecure. Without a strong middle class, the social fabric of the country begins to unravel, creating fertile ground for political instability, populism, and resentment.

The Permanent Underclass

At the bottom of the new corporate hierarchy is the **permanent underclass**, a growing population of workers who are increasingly trapped in low-wage jobs with no path to upward mobility. These workers—many of whom are people of color, immigrants, and women—make up the backbone of the service economy, performing essential work in industries like retail, food service, healthcare, and delivery. Yet despite the essential nature of their labor, they are paid poverty wages, offered no benefits, and given little job security.

In the medieval feudal system, peasants were bound to the land, working for their lords in exchange for protection and a place to live. Today's permanent underclass is similarly bound—not to the land, but to a system of **wage slavery** and **economic dependence** that keeps them in a perpetual state of insecurity. For these workers, the cost of living far exceeds their income, forcing them to rely on government assistance, charity, or multiple jobs just to survive.

The rise of the **gig economy** has played a major role in creating this new underclass. Companies like **DoorDash**, **Postmates**, and **Grubhub** have built multi-billion-dollar empires on the backs of gig workers who are classified as "independent contractors" rather than employees. This classification allows companies to avoid providing basic benefits like health insurance, paid leave, and retirement plans, while also denying workers the right to unionize. As a result, gig workers are forced to navigate a precarious job market where their income is inconsistent, their expenses are high, and their future is uncertain.

The lack of affordable **healthcare** and **housing** has further entrenched the permanent underclass. In a country where health insurance is tied to employment, millions of low-wage workers are left uninsured or underinsured, unable to afford basic medical care. A single illness or injury can plunge a family into financial ruin, trapping them in a cycle of debt and poverty. Meanwhile, the housing crisis has reached epic proportions, with rents skyrocketing in cities across the country and homeownership becoming increasingly out of reach. For many low-wage workers, the choice is between paying rent and buying food, with little hope of ever achieving financial stability.

Economic immobility is a defining feature of the permanent underclass. In previous generations, upward mobility was a realistic possibility for many workers, thanks to strong labor protections, affordable education, and accessible homeownership. But today, the pathways to upward mobility have been systematically dismantled, leaving millions of people trapped in low-wage jobs with no hope of advancement. The result is a system where economic inequality is not just a temporary condition—it is a permanent state of affairs, one in which the wealthy elite consolidate their power while the working poor are locked into a life of perpetual servitude.

The Return of Inequality

One of the most troubling aspects of neo-feudalism is the way in which economic inequality is used as a tool of **social control**. In medieval times, the nobility maintained their power by ensuring that the peasant class remained dependent on their lords for survival. Today, the corporate elite maintain their dominance through similar means, creating a system where the working class is so economically insecure that they cannot challenge the power structures that keep them in poverty.

Economic insecurity breeds **fear** and **compliance**. When workers are living paycheck to paycheck, burdened by debt, and struggling to afford basic necessities, they are far less likely to demand higher wages, better working conditions, or the right to unionize. Corporations have perfected the art of keeping workers desperate, knowing that a fearful and financially insecure workforce is easier to control. This is why corporations fight so fiercely against raising the minimum wage, providing healthcare, or offering paid leave—because they know that once workers are free from economic insecurity, they will begin to demand more from the system.

The extreme inequality that defines neo-feudalism also serves to divide the working class. By pitting workers against each other—whether it's through **racial**, **ethnic**, or **gender** divisions—corporations can prevent the kind of solidarity that would threaten their power. Workers who are focused on competing for scarce resources are less likely to unite in common cause, and this division ensures that the corporate lords can continue to extract wealth without facing organized resistance.

feudalism has created a society that is deeply divided along class lines, where a small corporate aristocracy holds all the power and wealth, while the rest of society is left to struggle for survival. The middle class, once a stabilizing force, is shrinking, while the permanent underclass grows larger and more desperate. This new hierarchy is not just a reflection of economic inequality—it is a deliberate system of control, designed to keep the working class in a state of dependence and submission.

The Corporate Takeover of Public Institutions

One of the most insidious ways that corporate power has embedded itself in the structures of governance is through the **privatization of public services**. Over the past several decades, governments—particularly in the United States—have increasingly outsourced essential public services to private corporations, allowing them to profit from services that were once the responsibility of the public sector. This shift toward privatization has been framed as a way to increase efficiency and reduce costs, but the reality is that it has turned vital services like education, healthcare, and infrastructure into lucrative profit centers for corporations, often with disastrous consequences for the public.

Take, for example, the privatization of **public education**. In many states, the rise of **charter schools**—privately run but publicly funded schools—has undermined traditional public education. Charter schools are often managed by for-profit companies that prioritize cost-cutting and profits over educational outcomes. These schools siphon funding away from traditional public schools, leaving them under-resourced and struggling to provide quality education to all students. While charter schools often promise better outcomes, studies have shown that they rarely deliver, and the children who suffer the most are those from low-income and marginalized communities.

Similarly, the **privatization of prisons** has created a perverse incentive structure in which private companies profit from mass incarceration. Private prison companies like **CoreCivic** and **GEO Group** have a vested interest in keeping prisons full, lobbying for tougher sentencing laws and policies that criminalize minor offenses. The result is a justice system that prioritizes profits over rehabilitation, turning prisoners into commodities in a system designed to extract maximum profit from their incarceration. This commodification of human lives is a hallmark of corporate feudalism, where even the most vulnerable members of society are seen as little more than revenue streams.

Privatization has also infiltrated public infrastructure. In many cities, essential services like water, energy, and public transportation have been handed over to private companies, often with disastrous consequences for consumers. The **Flint water crisis** is perhaps the most infamous example of what happens when public services are turned over to private contractors. In an effort to cut costs, Flint officials outsourced the city's water supply, leading to lead contamination that poisoned thousands of residents. This is the endgame of corporate governance: public welfare sacrificed at the altar of profit.

Lobbyists and Legislators

The privatization of public services is only one piece of the puzzle. At the heart of corporate feudalism is the ability of corporations to **directly influence the legislative process**, shaping laws and regulations to benefit their bottom lines. This is done through the overwhelming presence of **lobbyists**—well-paid professionals who work on behalf of corporations to push their agendas in the halls of government. Lobbying has become so entrenched in the political process that it is now virtually impossible to pass any significant piece of legislation without first securing the approval of corporate interests.

Lobbying is, at its core, a way for corporations to buy influence in government. While ordinary citizens have limited access to their representatives, corporations hire armies of lobbyists to ensure that their voices are heard loud and clear. These lobbyists spend billions each year meeting with lawmakers, drafting legislation, and ensuring that corporate-friendly policies are passed. Whether it's **Big Pharma** lobbying against drug price controls, **Big Oil** fighting climate regulations, or **tech giants** pushing for favorable tax policies, the legislative process has been hijacked by corporate money.

One of the most blatant examples of corporate influence over lawmaking is the role of **model legislation**—bills written by corporate lobbyists and then handed to lawmakers to introduce as their own. Organizations like the **American Legislative Exchange Council (ALEC)**, which is funded by major corporations, specialize in crafting these model bills, which are designed to benefit corporate donors. Whether it's bills that limit environmental protections, weaken labor laws, or strip away consumer rights, model legislation allows corporations to bypass the democratic process entirely, effectively writing the laws that govern us.

The revolving door between **corporate America** and **government** further cements the influence of corporations in lawmaking. Many former lawmakers and government officials go on to become lobbyists or take high-paying jobs in the industries they once regulated. This creates a conflict of interest, where government officials are incentivized to pass laws that favor the industries they hope to join once they leave public office. The result is a political system that is designed to serve corporate interests, not the public good.

Corporate Governance Over Democracy

As corporations have gained more power over public institutions, a new form of governance has emerged—**technocratic rule**, where decisions about public policy and economic management are increasingly handed over to unelected corporate elites. In this system, experts from the private sector are placed in positions of authority within government agencies, often under the assumption that their business acumen will make them more effective leaders than elected officials. This shift toward technocratic governance represents a dangerous trend, where corporate expertise is seen as more valuable than democratic accountability.

One of the clearest examples of this trend is the appointment of corporate executives to key government positions, where they are given broad authority to regulate the industries they come from. In recent years, numerous former executives from **Goldman Sachs, ExxonMobil**, and other major corporations have been appointed to high-level positions in the federal government, including the **Treasury Department, Environmental Protection Agency (EPA)**, and **Federal Communications Commission (FCC)**. These individuals bring with them a corporate mindset that prioritizes deregulation, privatization, and market-based solutions, often at the expense of public welfare.

This trend has been especially evident in the **regulatory capture** of agencies that are supposed to oversee industries like finance, energy, and telecommunications. Regulatory capture occurs when the agencies responsible for regulating an industry are co-opted by the very companies they are supposed to oversee. This allows corporations to essentially police themselves, with little oversight or accountability. The result is a system where industries like Wall Street, Big Pharma, and Big Oil are allowed to operate with minimal regulation, leading to financial crises, environmental disasters, and skyrocketing healthcare costs.

Corporate technocracy has also infiltrated international governance. Institutions like the **World Bank, International**

Monetary Fund (IMF), and **World Trade Organization (WTO)** are often dominated by corporate interests, pushing policies that benefit multinational corporations at the expense of workers, consumers, and the environment. These institutions promote **austerity measures, deregulation**, and **free trade agreements** that prioritize corporate profits over the needs of ordinary people. In many cases, governments in developing countries are forced to adopt these policies in exchange for financial aid, leading to widespread poverty, inequality, and environmental degradation.

The rise of technocratic rule represents a fundamental shift away from democratic governance. In a true democracy, elected representatives are accountable to the people who vote them into office. But in a technocracy, decisions are made by unelected corporate elites who have no accountability to the public. This shift not only undermines the democratic process but also concentrates power in the hands of a small, wealthy elite who are more interested in maximizing profits than in serving the public good.

The Erosion of Public Trust

The blurring of public and private power has had devastating consequences for public trust in democratic institutions. As more and more people come to see their governments as corrupt and beholden to corporate interests, faith in the democratic process is eroding. Voter turnout is declining, political polarization is increasing, and populist movements—both on the left and the right—are rising in response to the sense that democracy no longer works for ordinary people.

This crisis of democracy is not just a reflection of economic inequality—it is a direct result of corporate feudalism. When corporations are allowed to write laws, control public institutions, and dominate political discourse, the voices of ordinary citizens are drowned out. The result is a system that feels rigged, where elections seem meaningless and where the interests of the wealthy few always come before the needs of the many.

The rise of **corporate media** has further exacerbated this crisis. In today's media landscape, a handful of giant corporations control most of the news and information that the public consumes. Companies like **Comcast**, **Disney**, and **AT&T** dominate the media industry, shaping public discourse and controlling what issues get covered—and how. This consolidation of media power has made it increasingly difficult for independent journalism to thrive, leaving the public with fewer sources of unbiased information. Corporate media often serves as a mouthpiece for the interests of the wealthy elite, framing issues like climate change, healthcare reform, and economic inequality in ways that protect corporate profits.

The erosion of public trust is dangerous. Without faith in the democratic process, citizens become disillusioned and disengaged, allowing corporate power to grow unchecked. This creates a vicious cycle, where the more power corporations accumulate, the less influence ordinary people have over their own lives. Democracy, in this context, becomes little more than a façade—an illusion of choice in a system where the real decisions are made by unelected corporate elites.

The Battle for Democracy

The fusion of corporate power and public governance represents a fundamental threat to the future of democracy. As corporations continue to entrench themselves in the mechanisms of government, public institutions are being hollowed out, democratic accountability is being eroded, and the will of the people is increasingly subordinated to the interests of the wealthy elite. This is the defining feature of corporate feudalism—a system where the few rule over the many, not through military might, but through economic and political domination.

Global Domination and Corporate Imperialism

Economic Extraction

One of the most striking parallels between historical colonialism and modern corporate imperialism is the extraction of **natural resources** from the Global South. In the colonial era, European powers pillaged colonized lands for raw materials—gold, silver, spices, rubber, and more—fueling the wealth of empires while leaving local populations impoverished and disenfranchised. Today, multinational corporations continue this legacy of extraction, exploiting the natural wealth of developing nations while reaping enormous profits.

Corporations in industries such as **oil**, **mining**, **logging**, and **agriculture** have established a stranglehold on many of the world's most resource-rich regions, particularly in Africa, Latin America, and Southeast Asia. These corporations extract valuable resources—oil, minerals, timber, and cash crops—often with little regard for the environmental or social consequences. In many cases, they operate in partnership with corrupt or authoritarian governments that prioritize corporate interests over the well-being of their own citizens.

The **oil industry** is a prime example of how corporate imperialism operates in the Global South. In countries like **Nigeria**, **Ecuador**, and **Angola**, multinational oil companies like **ExxonMobil**, **Shell**, and **Chevron** have established a powerful presence, controlling vast reserves of oil while leaving local populations to deal with the fallout. In the Niger Delta, for instance, decades of oil extraction by Shell have led to widespread environmental devastation, including oil spills, pollution of water sources, and the destruction of local ecosystems. The indigenous communities who live in the Delta have seen little benefit from the oil wealth extracted from their land, while the profits flow to corporate headquarters in Europe and the United States.

This model of resource extraction is not unique to the oil industry. In the **mining sector**, multinational corporations like **Rio Tinto** and **Glencore** dominate the extraction of valuable minerals like copper, gold, and lithium, often in countries with weak environmental regulations and little oversight. These companies extract wealth from the land while leaving behind environmental destruction, contaminated water supplies, and health crises for local communities. The profits, of course, flow back to corporate shareholders in the Global North, while the people in the Global South are left with a legacy of poverty and ecological disaster.

The agricultural sector, too, has become a battleground for corporate imperialism. Global agribusiness giants like **Cargill**, **Monsanto (now owned by Bayer)**, and **Nestlé** control vast tracts of farmland in developing countries, often displacing local farmers and transforming diverse ecosystems into monoculture plantations for cash crops like soybeans, palm oil, and coffee. These crops are then exported to the Global North, where they fuel the processed food industry, while local populations are left with little access to their own land or food security.

In all of these cases, the extraction of natural resources from the Global South mirrors the patterns of historical colonialism. Just as European empires drained their colonies of wealth to enrich the mother country, today's multinational corporations extract resources from developing nations to enrich their shareholders. The result is a global economy that concentrates wealth and power in the hands of a few corporate elites, while leaving the Global South mired in poverty, environmental degradation, and economic dependency.

Labor Exploitation in the Global Supply Chain

Corporate imperialism is not only about the extraction of natural resources—it is also about the exploitation of **cheap labor** in the Global South. In the colonial era, European powers used enslaved or indentured labor to build their empires, forcing indigenous populations and enslaved Africans to work in mines, plantations, and factories under brutal conditions. Today, multinational corporations rely on a different kind of exploitation: the global supply chain, where workers in developing countries are paid poverty wages to produce goods for Western markets.

The **apparel** and **electronics** industries are two of the most notorious sectors for labor exploitation in the Global South. Corporations like **Nike**, **H&M**, **Apple**, and **Samsung** have outsourced the production of their goods to factories in countries like **Bangladesh**, **Vietnam**, **China**, and **India**, where labor is cheap and regulations are weak. In these factories, workers—many of them women and children—are paid poverty wages to work long hours in dangerous conditions. These workers often have little to no legal protections, and attempts to unionize or demand better conditions are frequently met with repression or violence.

The **Rana Plaza** disaster in Bangladesh in 2013, where over 1,100 garment workers were killed when a poorly constructed factory collapsed, is a stark reminder of the human cost of corporate imperialism. The factory was producing clothing for global brands like **Primark**, **Benetton**, and **Walmart**, all of which had outsourced production to Bangladesh to take advantage of its low wages and lax labor laws. After the disaster, it was revealed that workers had been forced to continue working in the building despite warnings about its structural integrity. This tragedy highlights the extreme risks faced by workers in the Global South, who are often treated as disposable by the corporations that profit from their labor.

In the **electronics** industry, labor exploitation takes a similar form. Factories in China, such as those owned by **Foxconn**, produce many of the world's most popular electronic devices, including iPhones, PlayStations, and Xboxes. Workers in these factories are subjected to grueling work schedules, low pay, and poor living conditions. Reports of worker suicides at Foxconn facilities prompted global outrage, but little has changed in terms of improving working conditions for the millions of laborers who produce electronics for the world's largest corporations.

This exploitation is facilitated by the global system of **free trade** and **outsourcing**, which allows corporations to move production to countries where wages are lowest and labor protections are weakest. The result is a global race to the bottom, where developing countries compete to attract foreign investment by offering lower wages, weaker environmental regulations, and fewer labor protections. This dynamic locks countries in the Global South into a cycle of dependency, where their economies are structured around providing cheap labor for global corporations rather than developing their own industries or improving the livelihoods of their citizens.

In many ways, this modern system of labor exploitation mirrors the practices of colonialism, where European powers extracted wealth from colonized populations while offering little in return. Today's multinational corporations extract value from the labor of workers in the Global South, while offering them poverty wages and few opportunities for advancement. The wealth generated from this exploitation flows back to the corporate headquarters in the Global North, further entrenching the economic inequality that defines corporate imperialism.

How Free Trade Traps the Global South

Corporate imperialism is sustained by a global economic system that keeps the nations of the Global South dependent on the markets, technologies, and capital of the Global North. This dependency is reinforced by the institutions of **global trade**, which are dominated by the interests of multinational corporations and the governments of wealthy nations. The **World Trade**

Organization (WTO), the International Monetary Fund (IMF), and the World Bank all play a central role in maintaining the global economic order, ensuring that developing nations remain subordinate to the demands of global capital.

One of the primary mechanisms through which corporate imperialism operates is the **free trade agreement (FTA)**. These agreements, which are often negotiated behind closed doors by corporate lobbyists and government officials, are designed to remove barriers to trade and investment, allowing multinational corporations to expand their operations in developing countries. While these agreements are often presented as beneficial to all parties, the reality is that they overwhelmingly favor the interests of corporations and wealthy nations, while undermining the sovereignty and economic independence of developing countries.

For example, trade agreements like the **North American Free Trade Agreement (NAFTA)** and the **Trans-Pacific Partnership (TPP)** have been criticized for allowing multinational corporations to exploit cheap labor in Mexico, Vietnam, and other developing countries, while offering little in the way of protections for workers or the environment. These agreements often include provisions that allow corporations to sue governments for regulations that limit their profits, effectively undermining the ability of nations to enact policies that protect their citizens or natural resources.

The **IMF** and the **World Bank** also play a key role in maintaining economic dependency in the Global South. These institutions provide loans to developing countries in exchange for the implementation of **structural adjustment programs (SAPs)**, which often include demands for austerity measures, privatization of public services, and the liberalization of trade. While these policies are intended to promote economic growth, they often have the opposite effect, deepening poverty and inequality while opening up markets for foreign corporations to exploit.

In many cases, countries in the Global South are forced to prioritize debt repayment over investments in healthcare, education, and infrastructure, leaving them trapped in a cycle of dependency. Meanwhile, multinational corporations continue to extract wealth from these nations, ensuring that they remain subordinate to the interests of global capital.

The result of this system is a global economy where the wealthiest nations and corporations control the rules of trade, while the nations of the Global South are locked into a subordinate position, providing cheap labor, raw materials, and markets for global corporations. This is the essence of corporate imperialism—an economic order that perpetuates inequality, environmental destruction, and social injustice, all in the service of maximizing profits for the world's most powerful corporations.

A New Era of Imperialism

Corporate imperialism represents a new era of global domination, where multinational corporations play the role once held by colonial empires. Through the extraction of resources, the exploitation of labor, and the perpetuation of economic dependency, these corporations have established a system of global control that mirrors the practices of historical colonialism. The nations of the Global South are left to bear the brunt of this exploitation, while the wealth flows to the Global North, enriching corporate elites and deepening global inequality.

Corporate Capture of the State

One of the most direct ways that multinational corporations exert control over governments in the Global South is through **corporate capture**—the process by which corporations infiltrate and co-opt public institutions, effectively turning governments into extensions of their own operations. Corporate capture can take many forms, from lobbying and financial influence to outright corruption and bribery. The goal is always the same: to ensure that governments prioritize corporate interests over public welfare.

In countries rich in natural resources, particularly in Africa and Latin America, multinational corporations often use their financial power to sway elections, lobby for favorable policies, and control key government institutions. For example, oil companies like **ExxonMobil** and **Chevron** have long been accused of exerting undue influence over the governments of countries like **Nigeria** and **Ecuador**, where they operate large-scale extraction projects. These companies have been implicated in bribing officials, funding political campaigns, and using their financial clout to shape regulations and policies that allow them to operate with minimal oversight.

In **Nigeria**, oil companies have a long history of influencing government policies to secure access to the country's vast oil reserves. The **Niger Delta**, which is home to much of Nigeria's oil wealth, has seen decades of environmental devastation and social unrest as a result of oil extraction by multinational companies like **Royal Dutch Shell**. Despite widespread protests by local communities, successive Nigerian governments have consistently prioritized the interests of these corporations over the needs of the population, often turning a blind eye to human rights abuses, environmental degradation, and corruption.

This dynamic is not limited to the oil industry. In **Brazil**, the **agricultural** and **mining** industries wield enormous influence over the government, with corporations like **Cargill** and **Vale** playing a key role in shaping policies that favor deforestation, land grabs, and resource extraction in the Amazon rainforest. These industries have lobbied aggressively against environmental protections and indigenous land rights, ensuring that the Brazilian government continues to prioritize corporate profits over the preservation of one of the world's most vital ecosystems.

In many cases, corporate capture is facilitated by **corruption**. Corporations offer bribes to politicians and officials to secure favorable contracts, regulatory exemptions, or preferential treatment. In return, governments turn a blind eye to corporate abuses, allowing companies to operate with impunity. This cycle of corruption not only undermines political sovereignty but also deepens the economic dependency of developing countries, as their governments become increasingly reliant on corporate investment and revenue streams.

The Rise of Corporate-Friendly Regimes

Corporate imperialism thrives in political environments where governments are either weak or authoritarian. In many cases, multinational corporations actively support or enable authoritarian regimes, knowing that these regimes are more likely to implement policies that favor corporate interests without the checks and balances of democratic governance. This creates a mutually beneficial relationship between authoritarian rulers and multinational corporations, where the latter provide financial backing, while the former ensure a stable, business-friendly environment.

One of the most prominent examples of this dynamic is the relationship between multinational corporations and the regime of **Hosni Mubarak** in **Egypt**. During Mubarak's 30-year reign, Egypt became a hub for multinational corporations seeking access to the Middle East and North Africa. Companies like **Coca-Cola**, **Procter & Gamble**, and **BP** thrived under Mubarak's regime, benefiting from policies that prioritized foreign investment and deregulation. In return, these corporations helped prop up Mubarak's authoritarian rule, which was characterized by widespread human rights abuses, political repression, and economic inequality. The **Arab Spring** uprisings that eventually toppled Mubarak were fueled in part by frustration with the economic disparities that had been exacerbated by corporate-friendly policies.

A similar pattern can be seen in **Kazakhstan**, where the authoritarian government of **Nursultan Nazarbayev** maintained close ties with multinational oil and gas companies. Kazakhstan, which sits on some of the world's largest oil and natural gas reserves, attracted billions of dollars in foreign investment from companies like **Chevron** and **ExxonMobil**. These corporations benefited from Kazakhstan's lax environmental regulations and weak labor protections, while the Nazarbayev regime used corporate revenues to consolidate power, suppress dissent, and maintain a tight grip on the country's political system.

The rise of corporate-friendly authoritarian regimes is not confined to the oil-rich nations of Africa and Central Asia. In countries like **Indonesia, the Philippines**, and **Honduras**, multinational corporations have supported or benefited from governments that suppress labor rights, criminalize environmental activism, and silence opposition. In these countries, corporate interests are often aligned with authoritarian rulers who see civil liberties and democratic institutions as obstacles to business. As a result, multinational corporations become complicit in the erosion of democracy and the violation of human rights.

Authoritarian regimes are particularly attractive to multinational corporations because they provide stability—at least from a corporate perspective. In these countries, there is little risk of regulatory changes, labor strikes, or environmental protests disrupting business operations. Corporations can operate with minimal scrutiny, knowing that governments will prioritize their interests over those of the population. This mutually beneficial arrangement, however, comes at a steep cost for the people living under these regimes, who are often left without a voice or the ability to challenge the exploitation of their country's resources and labor.

The Consequences of Corporate Control: Erosion of Political Sovereignty and Democratic Institutions

The political influence of multinational corporations has far-reaching consequences for the sovereignty and democratic institutions of countries in the Global South. As corporations capture governments, promote corporate-friendly regimes, and manipulate the political system to their advantage, the ability of these countries to govern themselves in the interests of their citizens is severely compromised. This erosion of political sovereignty undermines democracy, weakens public institutions, and deepens inequality.

One of the most significant consequences of corporate control is the **privatization** of public services and infrastructure, a trend that has accelerated in many developing countries under pressure from multinational corporations and international financial institutions. Privatization often leads to higher costs and lower-quality services for ordinary citizens, as private companies prioritize profits over public welfare. In many cases, the privatization of essential services like water, energy, and healthcare disproportionately affects the poorest members of society, who are often priced out of access to basic necessities.

For example, in **Bolivia**, the privatization of the water supply in the city of **Cochabamba** sparked widespread protests in 2000, known as the **Water War**. The Bolivian government, under pressure from the **World Bank**, had handed control of the city's water supply to a private consortium led by the multinational company **Bechtel**. The company promptly raised water prices to unaffordable levels, leading to a public outcry and violent clashes between protesters and security forces. In the end, the government was forced to reverse the privatization, but the incident highlighted the dangers of corporate control over essential public services.

The erosion of political sovereignty is also evident in the **legal mechanisms** that multinational corporations use to protect their interests. Through **investor-state dispute settlement (ISDS)** clauses in trade agreements, corporations can sue governments for implementing regulations that they claim harm their profits. These legal mechanisms allow corporations to bypass domestic courts and hold governments accountable in international arbitration tribunals, often resulting in massive payouts to corporations at the expense of taxpayers.

One high-profile example of this occurred in **Ecuador**, where the oil company **Chevron** was sued by indigenous communities for environmental damages caused by decades of oil extraction in the Amazon rainforest. After losing the case in Ecuadorian courts, Chevron turned to international arbitration, using an ISDS mechanism to challenge the ruling. In 2018, the arbitration tribunal ruled in Chevron's favor, ordering Ecuador's government to pay millions in compensation to the company, even though the original court ruling had found Chevron responsible for widespread environmental destruction. This case highlights the ways in which corporate power can override national sovereignty and undermine the ability of governments to hold corporations accountable for their actions.

The consequences of corporate control go beyond economic and legal issues. In many countries, the influence of multinational corporations has contributed to the **criminalization of dissent** and the suppression of civil society. Environmental activists, labor organizers, and indigenous leaders who challenge corporate interests are often targeted for harassment, imprisonment, or even assassination. In countries like **Honduras** and **the Philippines**, violence against activists is widespread, with corporations and governments working hand in hand to silence opposition.

The erosion of democratic institutions is perhaps the most damaging consequence of corporate imperialism. As multinational corporations capture governments and promote authoritarian regimes, the voices of ordinary citizens are marginalized, and democratic participation becomes increasingly meaningless. In many countries, elections are little more than a formality, with corporate-backed candidates dominating the political landscape and opposition parties struggling to gain traction. The result is a political system that serves the interests of global capital rather than the needs of the people.

Resource Extraction and Environmental Degradation

At the heart of corporate imperialism lies the **extraction of natural resources**, a practice that devastates ecosystems and leaves lasting scars on the environment. Multinational corporations in industries such as oil, mining, and agriculture have become infamous for their role in stripping the land of its resources with little regard for the environmental consequences. These corporations often operate in countries with weak environmental regulations or corrupt governments, allowing them to maximize profits while minimizing accountability for the damage they cause.

One of the most egregious examples of this is the **Amazon rainforest**, often referred to as the "lungs of the planet" for its role in producing oxygen and regulating the global climate. Over the past few decades, the Amazon has become a key battleground in the fight against corporate environmental destruction. Global agribusiness giants, such as **Cargill** and **JBS**, have been instrumental in clearing vast swaths of the rainforest to make way for cattle ranching, soybean plantations, and palm oil production. This deforestation not only destroys one of the most biodiverse ecosystems on Earth, but also contributes to climate change by releasing massive amounts of carbon dioxide into the atmosphere.

The devastation of the Amazon is not an isolated incident. Across Latin America, Africa, and Southeast Asia, corporations engage in similar practices, driven by the demand for raw materials in the Global North. In **Indonesia** and **Malaysia**, palm oil plantations have led to the widespread destruction of tropical rainforests, threatening species such as orangutans and Sumatran tigers while displacing indigenous communities. The environmental destruction caused by palm oil production has also contributed to **massive fires**, releasing toxic smoke that affects millions of people across Southeast Asia.

The mining industry is another key driver of environmental degradation in the Global South. Corporations like **Rio Tinto**, **BHP**, and **Barrick Gold** extract valuable minerals such as copper, gold, and rare earth elements from some of the world's most ecologically sensitive areas. These mining operations often lead to deforestation, water contamination, and habitat destruction. In countries like **Peru, the Democratic Republic of Congo (DRC)**, and **Papua New Guinea**, local communities have been left with polluted rivers, toxic waste, and degraded farmland as a result of corporate mining activities. These communities often suffer the worst consequences of environmental destruction while seeing little to no economic benefit from the extraction of their natural resources.

Oil extraction is perhaps the most visible and destructive form of resource exploitation in the Global South. In regions like the **Niger Delta** in Nigeria and the **Ecuadorian Amazon**, multinational oil companies have engaged in practices that have caused environmental catastrophes. Oil spills, gas flaring, and pipeline leaks have contaminated water supplies, destroyed farmland, and caused widespread health problems for local populations. In the Niger Delta, decades of oil extraction by companies like **Shell** and **Chevron** have left the region's ecosystems in ruins, with oil spills coating rivers and wetlands in toxic sludge. Indigenous communities, whose livelihoods depend on fishing and agriculture, have been left with little recourse, as the Nigerian government has consistently sided with the oil companies.

The environmental consequences of these extractive industries are not just local—they are global. The destruction of tropical rainforests, which act as vital carbon sinks, and the release of greenhouse gases from mining and oil extraction contribute to the **global climate crisis**, which disproportionately affects the world's poorest and most vulnerable populations. The exploitation of natural resources in the Global South is one of the driving forces behind climate change, yet the countries most responsible for this environmental destruction—corporations headquartered in the Global North—rarely bear the consequences.

Displacement and Exploitation of Indigenous Communities

The environmental destruction wrought by corporate imperialism often comes at the direct expense of **indigenous communities**, who are displaced from their ancestral lands and left to deal with the aftermath of corporate extraction. These communities, which have lived in harmony with their environments for centuries, find themselves on the front lines of corporate exploitation, facing displacement, loss of livelihoods, and even violence at the hands of corporate-backed governments and security forces.

Indigenous communities are often the first to feel the impacts of deforestation, mining, and oil extraction, as their lands are frequently targeted by multinational corporations seeking to extract resources. These communities are rarely consulted about corporate activities on their lands, and when they resist, they are often met with violent repression. In **Brazil**, indigenous leaders who have opposed deforestation and land grabs in the Amazon have been murdered by illegal loggers and land speculators, many of whom have ties to large agribusiness corporations. The **Kayapo** and other indigenous groups in the Amazon have been fighting for decades to protect their lands from destruction, but corporate interests, backed by powerful political allies, have consistently undermined their efforts.

The displacement of indigenous communities is not limited to the Amazon. In **Papua New Guinea**, mining projects operated by companies like **Rio Tinto** and **BHP** have forced indigenous peoples off their land, polluting rivers and destroying ecosystems that these communities rely on for their survival. In the **Philippines**, indigenous groups fighting against mining operations and deforestation have faced intimidation, violence, and forced displacement by both corporate-backed militias and government forces. These communities are often left with little recourse, as legal systems in many countries are stacked against them, favoring corporate interests over the rights of indigenous peoples.

The displacement and exploitation of indigenous communities is not only a human rights issue—it is also an environmental issue. Indigenous peoples are often the best stewards of their environments, managing land and resources sustainably through traditional ecological knowledge. By displacing these communities, corporations not only destroy the cultural heritage of indigenous peoples but also contribute to the degradation of ecosystems that have been sustainably managed for generations. This destruction is irreversible in many cases, as once these ecosystems are lost, they cannot be restored to their previous state.

In addition to displacement, indigenous communities often bear the brunt of **environmental racism**—the unequal distribution of environmental harms. Toxic waste from mining, oil extraction, and industrial agriculture is frequently dumped in or near indigenous lands, contaminating water supplies, poisoning soil, and causing severe health problems. In many cases, indigenous communities are left with little recourse to seek justice, as corporations and governments collude to cover up environmental crimes and suppress dissent.

Climate Change and Corporate Responsibility

The global climate crisis is inextricably linked to corporate imperialism, as the activities of multinational corporations—particularly in the fossil fuel and extractive industries—are some of the primary drivers of climate change. Corporate practices that prioritize short-term profits over environmental sustainability have resulted in the emission of massive amounts of **greenhouse gases**, deforestation, and the degradation of ecosystems that act as natural carbon sinks. Despite overwhelming scientific consensus about the dangers of climate change, many multinational corporations continue to engage in practices that exacerbate the problem, all while attempting to deflect responsibility for their role in the crisis.

Fossil fuel companies, in particular, bear a significant share of responsibility for climate change. A 2017 report by the **Carbon Majors Database** revealed that just **100 companies** are responsible for over **70%** of global greenhouse gas emissions since 1988, with oil giants like **ExxonMobil**, **Shell**, and **BP** at the top of the list. These corporations have spent decades lobbying against climate regulations, funding climate denial campaigns, and undermining global efforts to transition to renewable energy. At the same time, they continue to expand oil and gas production in some of the world's most vulnerable regions, from the Arctic to the Amazon, with little regard for the long-term environmental consequences.

The impact of climate change is already being felt across the globe, but it is the poorest and most vulnerable communities—particularly those in the Global South—that are bearing the brunt of the crisis. Rising sea levels, extreme weather events, and shifting agricultural patterns are threatening the livelihoods of millions of people in developing countries, many of whom are the least responsible for global greenhouse gas emissions. **Pacific Island nations** like **Tuvalu** and **Kiribati** are facing the prospect of becoming uninhabitable due to rising sea levels, while **Sub-Saharan Africa** is experiencing more frequent droughts, putting millions at risk of food insecurity.

Despite the overwhelming evidence of corporate responsibility for climate change, many multinational corporations have attempted to **greenwash** their public image by making token commitments to sustainability while continuing to engage in environmentally destructive practices. Companies like **BP** and **Chevron** have launched advertising campaigns promoting their investments in renewable energy, even as they continue to invest billions in oil and gas exploration. This form of corporate hypocrisy—claiming to be part of the solution while remaining part of the problem—has slowed global progress on climate action and allowed corporations to continue profiting from the destruction of the planet.

As the climate crisis accelerates, the need for corporate accountability has never been more urgent. Multinational corporations must be held responsible for their role in driving climate change, and governments must enact strong regulations to curb the worst practices of the fossil fuel industry and other environmentally destructive sectors. Without significant changes to the way corporations operate, the global climate crisis will continue to deepen, with catastrophic consequences for the world's most vulnerable populations.

The Struggle Forward

The global stranglehold that corporations have on our lives, our lands, and our futures has reached a breaking point. For too long, multinational corporations have acted with impunity, stripping the world of its resources, exploiting its people, and bulldozing over any semblance of local democracy. But the tide is beginning to turn. Around the world, a wave of **grassroots resistance** is rising—a groundswell of anger, frustration, and fury aimed squarely at the corporate powers that have for too long been allowed to dictate the terms of life on this planet.

These movements aren't waiting for corporate elites to wake up to the harm they're causing. They aren't patiently asking for reforms. They are **fighting back**—with protests, blockades, legal battles, and direct action, reclaiming power from the corporations that have waged economic, political, and environmental war on the working people of the world. This is a battle for survival, and the message is clear: the age of corporate imperialism is being met with a resistance that is fierce, organized, and unafraid.

Defending the Land Against Corporate Plunder

Corporations may think they own the world's natural resources, but they didn't count on the fierce resistance of the people who actually live on and depend on those lands. **Indigenous groups**, rural communities, and environmental activists have emerged as some of the most fearless and tenacious opponents of corporate exploitation, often risking their lives to protect their land, water, and way of life from being swallowed up by multinational giants.

In the Amazon rainforest, indigenous communities have faced down some of the largest and most powerful corporations on the planet in their battle to protect their ancestral lands. The **Kayapo** people, led by the legendary chief **Raoni Metuktire**, have been on the front lines of the fight against deforestation for decades. They've gone head-to-head with agribusiness giants, illegal loggers, and mining companies that see the rainforest as nothing more than a resource to be pillaged for profit. Their resistance has ranged from legal battles in international courts to physical blockades, where entire villages have stood in the path of bulldozers and logging trucks to protect the forest.

These are not just isolated skirmishes—they are part of a global war on corporate environmental destruction. In **Standing Rock**, North Dakota, the **Dakota Access Pipeline (DAPL)** became a flashpoint for indigenous resistance against corporate greed and environmental degradation. The Standing Rock Sioux tribe, backed by thousands of supporters, launched a monumental campaign to stop the construction of an oil pipeline that threatened their water supply and sacred lands. Despite violent repression from the state, the movement gained international attention and mobilized solidarity protests around the world. The DAPL fight wasn't just about a single pipeline; it was about the right of indigenous communities to have a say in what happens to their lands—a right corporations have systematically ignored.

These communities understand what's at stake. They aren't just fighting for abstract environmental ideals; they are fighting for their very survival. **When a river is poisoned by oil spills, when forests are cleared for palm plantations, when mountaintops are blown away for coal**, entire communities are left devastated, with no means of sustaining themselves. Corporate executives sitting in boardrooms half a world away may not give a damn about the consequences of their actions, but the people on the ground do, and they are not backing down.

The resistance to corporate environmental plunder isn't limited to indigenous communities. Across the globe, ordinary citizens are rising up to defend their local environments against the corporate machine. In places like **Flint, Michigan**, residents have fought tooth and nail against a corporate-backed government decision that poisoned their water supply with lead. The **Flint Water Crisis** was a stark example of how corporate negligence and government complicity can devastate communities, and the people of Flint have refused to let those responsible walk away unscathed. Despite years of cover-ups and denials, grassroots organizing has kept the pressure on local and state officials, demanding accountability and justice for the victims.

In **South Africa**, rural communities have mobilized against coal mining corporations that are ravaging the environment and endangering the health of local residents. In **Somkhele**, local women have led the charge against the expansion of coal mines, which have polluted water sources, destroyed farmland, and displaced entire villages. They have staged protests, blockaded mining operations, and taken their fight to the courts, determined to protect their communities from the environmental and economic devastation wrought by corporate mining interests.

These are not passive victims of corporate greed—they are warriors, fighting for the future of their lands, their families, and the planet itself. The corporations may have money and power, but these grassroots movements have something far more important: **righteous fury** and the moral authority of defending the earth against its destruction.

Workers Revolt Against Corporate Exploitation

While corporations celebrate record profits and obscene bonuses for their executives, the workers who generate that wealth are fed up, exhausted, and done playing nice. Across the world, workers are rising up in rebellion against the corporations that have built their empires on the backs of exploited labor. From the Amazon warehouses of the United States to the garment factories of Bangladesh, from the gig workers in Europe to miners in South Africa, workers are organizing, striking, and demanding justice from the corporations that have systematically abused them for profit.

    The corporate overlords never imagined that their low-paid, overworked labor force would fight back—but they underestimated just how much anger they've created. In the United States, **Amazon**, one of the most notoriously exploitative companies in the world, has become the center of a growing labor movement. Amazon workers are subjected to brutal working conditions in warehouses, where they are pushed to meet impossible quotas, denied bathroom breaks, and constantly monitored by surveillance technology that treats them like robots. In 2021, workers in **Bessemer, Alabama** attempted to form a union, a historic effort that drew international attention and mobilized support from labor activists across the globe.

    Although the initial union vote in Bessemer failed—thanks in no small part to Amazon's vicious anti-union campaign—the fight is far from over. The effort sparked a wave of organizing across the country, as workers in Amazon facilities from **New York** to **California** have started to demand their rights. The company's obscene profits, generated during the COVID-19 pandemic, have only fueled the anger of workers who have been forced to risk their lives in unsafe conditions while Amazon's executives reap billions. The workers are sending a clear message: **We're not your slaves, and we won't be treated like disposable machines**.

    This wave of labor rebellion isn't confined to the U.S. In **Bangladesh**, garment workers, who produce clothes for some of the world's biggest brands like **H&M**, **Zara**, and **Primark**, have taken to the streets in protest of poverty wages, unsafe working conditions, and rampant exploitation. The 2013 **Rana Plaza** disaster, in which over 1,100 garment workers were killed when a factory collapsed, exposed the brutal conditions that underpin the fashion industry's profits. Despite promises of reform, little has changed for the workers who are still paid starvation wages to make clothing for the Global North. But these workers are no longer willing to be exploited in silence. They've organized strikes, staged walkouts, and forced brands to answer for their role in maintaining this system of abuse.

The **gig economy**—hailed by corporations as a new frontier of "flexible" work—has become a flashpoint for labor resistance as well. Companies like **Uber, Lyft,** and **DoorDash** have built multi-billion-dollar empires by exploiting gig workers, who are denied basic benefits like healthcare, sick leave, and job security. These companies have fought tooth and nail to classify workers as "independent contractors," a label that strips them of the legal protections afforded to traditional employees. But gig workers are fighting back, from organizing in **California** to protests in **London** and **Barcelona**. They are demanding recognition as workers with rights, not disposable cogs in a profit machine.

This is the **workers' revolution** that corporations have long feared. After decades of union-busting, wage suppression, and brutal working conditions, workers are no longer willing to accept their fate. They are organizing in warehouses, fast-food restaurants, tech companies, and gig platforms, demanding better pay, safer conditions, and a voice in the workplace. The days of passive labor exploitation are over—the workers are fighting back, and they are not asking for permission.

Communities Fight Corporate Gentrification and Economic Exploitation

Corporations are not only exploiting labor and resources—they're also gentrifying entire communities, turning neighborhoods into playgrounds for the wealthy while displacing working-class residents who can no longer afford to live there. This process of **corporate gentrification** has sparked fierce resistance from communities across the world, where residents are fighting to reclaim their neighborhoods from the corporate developers, landlords, and investors who are driving up rents and pushing people out of their homes.

In cities like **San Francisco**, **New York**, and **London**, corporate tech giants and real estate developers have turned once-vibrant working-class neighborhoods into overpriced luxury enclaves for the wealthy elite. The arrival of companies like **Google**, **Facebook**, and **Amazon** has driven up housing prices to astronomical levels, forcing long-time residents to leave and erasing the cultural fabric of entire communities. But the people who built these neighborhoods are fighting back against the corporate gentrification machine.

In **Oakland, California**, a city that has become a battleground for gentrification, residents have organized tenant unions, staged rent strikes, and fought corporate landlords who are jacking up rents and evicting tenants. The **Moms 4 Housing** movement, in which a group of homeless mothers took over a vacant, investor-owned home in West Oakland, sparked a national conversation about the right to housing and the damage caused by corporate real estate speculation. These women refused to accept the idea that homes could sit empty while people were left on the streets, and their bold act of resistance forced the city and corporate developers to confront the human cost of gentrification.

In **New York City**, where the cost of living has skyrocketed thanks to corporate-driven real estate development, tenant groups and housing activists have fought back against the powerful landlords and developers who treat housing as a commodity rather than a human right. Groups like **Housing Justice for All** have mobilized renters to demand stronger rent control laws, eviction moratoriums, and affordable housing. They have staged protests, taken over city council meetings, and built coalitions with labor unions and environmental groups to challenge the unchecked power of corporate developers.

These community resistance movements are sending a clear message: **Our neighborhoods are not for sale**. Corporations and real estate speculators may see profits in gentrification, but these communities see displacement, cultural erasure, and economic exploitation. The fight for housing justice is a fight against corporate power, and it's one that communities across the world are waging with increasing ferocity.

The People Strike Back

Grassroots resistance is a growing force in the battle against corporate imperialism. Whether it's the defense of indigenous lands, the revolt of exploited workers, or the fight to reclaim gentrified neighborhoods, ordinary people are standing up to corporate tyranny in ways that are loud, angry, and unapologetic. These movements aren't waiting for permission or reform—they are demanding change through direct action, organizing, and resistance.

The Power of Disruption

The rise of grassroots resistance against corporate imperialism isn't just a spontaneous uprising—it's a calculated, strategic fight designed to dismantle the oppressive systems that multinational corporations have built to exploit the world. These aren't desperate acts of rebellion; they are organized, relentless, and increasingly sophisticated efforts to wrest control back from the corporate elite. The battleground spans multiple fronts—protests, blockades, legal battles, boycotts, and digital warfare—all aimed at forcing corporations to answer for the harm they've inflicted on people, communities, and the environment.

As corporations become more powerful, so too does the resistance against them. In this section, we will explore the various strategies that grassroots movements and activists have deployed in their fight against corporate domination. These strategies range from **direct action** and civil disobedience to **legal challenges** that push corporations into the courtroom, where they must face public scrutiny for their crimes. What unites these efforts is a burning rage against the unchecked power of the corporate oligarchy and a determination to bring it to its knees.

One of the most effective and visible forms of resistance against corporate imperialism is **direct action**. Direct action goes beyond protests and petitions; it is about directly disrupting corporate operations, forcing companies to confront the damage they're causing and often costing them millions in lost revenue. This form of resistance has been at the heart of many of the world's most significant movements against corporate power, and it has proven time and again that ordinary people, when organized, can take on the biggest corporations in the world.

Blockades, sit-ins, and occupations have been used by environmental activists, labor organizers, and social justice movements to disrupt the flow of business for corporations that refuse to listen to demands for change. In the United States, the **Standing Rock** protests against the Dakota Access Pipeline were a prime example of direct action on a massive scale. Thousands of indigenous activists, environmentalists, and allies gathered at the construction site, physically blocking the pipeline's progress. The protest camps became a flashpoint for the larger struggle against fossil fuel extraction, drawing international attention and forcing corporate and political elites to reckon with the power of direct action.

The tactics used at Standing Rock echoed a long history of environmental direct action. **Earth First!**, a radical environmental group, pioneered the use of **tree-sitting** to block logging operations in the Pacific Northwest in the 1980s and 1990s. Activists would physically occupy trees, preventing logging companies from cutting them down and bringing corporate destruction to a halt. These tree-sits were dangerous and often met with violent repression by law enforcement, but they were effective in delaying or even halting logging operations. The strategy worked not only by directly stopping corporate exploitation but also by drawing media attention to environmental destruction that would otherwise have gone unnoticed.

Direct action has also been a critical tool for **labor movements** fighting against corporate exploitation. In countries like **France** and **Italy**, workers have a long tradition of militant direct action, including factory occupations and general strikes. When French workers at **Goodyear** faced the closure of their factory, they responded with a series of strikes and factory occupations, culminating in a high-profile incident where workers held two managers hostage, demanding better severance packages. This tactic of **bossnapping**—while controversial—demonstrated the lengths to which workers were willing to go to protect their livelihoods in the face of corporate greed. In the end, Goodyear was forced to make concessions, proving once again that direct action can have real, tangible results.

Across the world, activists are turning to **disruption tactics** as a means of fighting corporate imperialism. In **Chile**, protests against corporate-backed government austerity measures and inequality led to nationwide strikes and the occupation of public spaces. In **Colombia**, indigenous groups have used road blockades to stop mining operations and call attention to the environmental and social devastation caused by corporate extractivism. These acts of resistance are often met with brutal crackdowns, but they continue to grow in scale and intensity, as more people recognize that direct action is one of the most powerful tools they have in the fight against corporate power.

Legal Warfare

While direct action disrupts business operations on the ground, legal challenges are another crucial battleground in the fight against corporate imperialism. For years, corporations have relied on their vast wealth and legal teams to evade accountability, using complex legal frameworks and arbitration clauses to shield themselves from lawsuits. But activists and lawyers have begun turning these same legal systems against the corporations, filing lawsuits that expose corporate wrongdoing, force regulatory change, and, in some cases, deliver financial penalties.

One of the most significant examples of legal resistance is the **Chevron-Ecuador case**, where indigenous communities from the Ecuadorian Amazon filed a lawsuit against **Chevron** for environmental destruction caused by decades of oil extraction. Chevron's operations, inherited from its acquisition of **Texaco**, left behind massive oil spills, contaminated water sources, and devastated ecosystems, with devastating health consequences for the local population. After years of legal battles, the indigenous plaintiffs won a historic $9.5 billion judgment against Chevron in Ecuadorian courts.

However, Chevron refused to pay, and the company fought back with a massive legal counteroffensive, using **corporate-friendly international arbitration** to overturn the ruling and launch a personal vendetta against the lawyers and activists involved in the case. While Chevron has successfully evaded financial accountability so far, the legal case exposed the corporation's dirty tactics and generated international outrage, rallying activists around the world. It also highlighted the growing use of international courts and **investor-state dispute settlements (ISDS)** by corporations to shield themselves from domestic accountability—a legal system that activists are now working to reform.

In a similar vein, **Shell** has faced a wave of legal challenges for its role in **Nigeria**, where its oil operations have led to devastating environmental damage in the Niger Delta. In 2021, a Dutch court ruled that Shell was responsible for oil spills in Nigeria and ordered the company to compensate affected communities. This case was significant not only because it held a major multinational accountable for its actions abroad, but also because it set a legal precedent for using home-country courts to sue corporations for actions taken in other countries. This victory opens the door for more lawsuits against corporations in their home countries, where the legal frameworks are often more robust and less corrupt than in the nations they exploit.

Climate litigation has also become a powerful tool in the battle against corporate imperialism. In recent years, activists and lawyers have launched lawsuits against fossil fuel companies, accusing them of knowingly contributing to climate change and misleading the public about the environmental damage caused by their operations. In 2015, a groundbreaking case in the Netherlands resulted in a court ordering the Dutch government to reduce greenhouse gas emissions by 25%, a ruling that set off a wave of climate litigation across Europe. In the U.S., several states and municipalities have sued oil companies like **ExxonMobil**, claiming they deceived the public about the dangers of climate change for decades while continuing to pollute the environment. These lawsuits have the potential to reshape the legal landscape, holding corporations accountable for their role in the climate crisis.

Legal warfare is not limited to environmental cases. Labor movements have used legal challenges to fight back against corporate exploitation, particularly in the gig economy. In California, a group of gig workers sued **Uber** and **Lyft**, challenging the companies' classification of workers as "independent contractors" rather than employees. This classification allows companies to deny workers benefits like healthcare, sick leave, and job security. The legal battle culminated in the passage of **Proposition 22**, a controversial ballot initiative backed by tech companies that overturned a state law designed to classify gig workers as employees. Despite the setback, the legal fight continues, with labor activists using lawsuits to challenge corporate practices that undermine worker rights.

These legal challenges are critical because they force corporations into the public spotlight, exposing their practices and holding them accountable in ways that direct action alone often cannot. While the legal system is far from perfect—and often biased in favor of corporate power—it remains one of the key arenas in which activists can fight back against corporate imperialism.

Boycotts, Divestment, and Consumer Power

In the face of corporate domination, one of the most powerful tools of resistance available to the public is the **boycott**. Boycotts have a long history as a form of protest against unjust corporations, leveraging consumer power to hurt companies where it matters most: their bottom line. By refusing to buy products, use services, or invest in companies that engage in unethical practices, ordinary people can force corporations to change their behavior or face significant financial losses.

One of the most successful examples of a boycott in recent history is the **Boycott, Divestment, and Sanctions (BDS)** movement, which aims to put economic pressure on corporations that profit from the Israeli occupation of Palestine. The BDS movement has targeted companies like **Caterpillar**, **HP**, and **G4S**, which provide equipment, technology, and services used by the Israeli government to maintain control over the occupied territories. By encouraging consumers, institutions, and governments to stop doing business with these corporations, the BDS movement has been able to draw international attention to the role of corporate complicity in human rights abuses, while also pressuring companies to reconsider their involvement in the occupation.

Divestment has also become a key strategy in the fight against climate change, with activists pushing institutions like universities, pension funds, and governments to divest from fossil fuel companies. The **Fossil Free** movement has successfully pressured major institutions, including the **University of California** and **Norway's sovereign wealth fund**, to pull billions of dollars out of fossil fuel investments. While divestment alone won't solve the climate crisis, it sends a powerful message to corporations that their business model is no longer acceptable in a world facing ecological collapse.

Boycotts have also been used to challenge corporate abuses in labor and human rights. In the 1990s, activists launched a global boycott of **Nike**, which had become notorious for using sweatshop labor in its factories across Asia. The boycott, coupled with direct action and media campaigns, forced Nike to change its labor practices, although the company still faces criticism for its supply chain practices today. More recently, boycotts against companies like **Nestlé**, **Amazon**, and **Uber** have gained traction, as consumers increasingly demand ethical practices from the corporations they do business with.

The success of boycotts and divestment campaigns lies in their ability to target corporate profits directly. Corporations may be able to ignore protests and legal challenges, but when their revenue streams start to dry up, they are forced to pay attention. While no single boycott is likely to bring a corporation to its knees, the cumulative effect of sustained economic pressure can force companies to make concessions or change their practices to protect their bottom line.

A Growing Arsenal of Resistance

From direct action to legal warfare, boycotts to divestment, the strategies used by grassroots movements and activists to fight corporate imperialism are diverse, innovative, and increasingly effective. These tactics aim to disrupt, expose, and undermine the power of multinational corporations, holding them accountable for their abuses and challenging the systems that allow them to operate with impunity. The fight against corporate domination is being waged on multiple fronts, and as these strategies evolve, so too does the movement's ability to push back against corporate greed and exploitation.

The Global Workers' Movement

Perhaps the most powerful and long-standing form of transnational solidarity has come from the **labor movement**. Workers around the world are connected through global supply chains that allow corporations to exploit low-wage labor in one country while selling goods in another. While corporations thrive on this division, workers are increasingly seeing the power in organizing across borders. The rise of **global unions** and international labor alliances has given workers a new set of tools to challenge corporate exploitation, especially in industries like manufacturing, retail, and technology.

A prime example of global labor solidarity is the **Global Union Federations (GUFs)**, which bring together national labor unions from across the world to coordinate their efforts against multinational corporations. One of the most significant victories for international labor came in 2013, after the **Rana Plaza** disaster in Bangladesh, when over 1,100 garment workers were killed in the collapse of a factory producing clothing for Western brands. In the aftermath, global unions like **IndustriALL** and **UNI Global Union** teamed up with Bangladeshi labor leaders to pressure corporations into signing the **Bangladesh Accord on Fire and Building Safety**, a legally binding agreement that forced brands to take responsibility for working conditions in their supply chains.

The success of the Bangladesh Accord wasn't just a win for garment workers—it was a blueprint for how labor movements could leverage their global strength to hold corporations accountable. By coordinating boycotts, strikes, and public pressure campaigns in countries where the brands were based, international unions and activists forced corporations to act. This kind of global solidarity is becoming increasingly common as workers recognize that their struggle is not confined to their own borders.

Amazon has become another focal point for transnational labor organizing. Workers from Amazon warehouses in **Germany**, **Italy**, **Spain**, and **France** have organized strikes and protests, often coordinating their efforts to maximize disruption across the company's global supply chain. These actions have been supported by global labor groups, such as the **International Transport Workers' Federation (ITF)**, which represents warehouse and logistics workers around the world. In 2020, during the COVID-19 pandemic, Amazon workers across multiple countries staged walkouts to protest unsafe working conditions and the lack of hazard pay. This show of international solidarity put pressure on Amazon, a company notorious for its anti-union practices, and demonstrated the growing power of global labor alliances.

The fight for labor rights in the **gig economy** is another arena where global alliances are taking shape. Gig workers from **Uber**, **Deliveroo**, and **Lyft** are connecting with labor organizers in multiple countries to demand better pay, job security, and benefits. In 2021, gig workers from across Europe organized a coordinated strike on **International Workers' Day**, calling for an end to precarious working conditions and the misclassification of gig workers as independent contractors. The solidarity shown between workers in **Italy**, **Spain**, **the UK**, and other countries represents a new phase in labor organizing—one that transcends national boundaries and targets the global business models that exploit workers.

While global labor organizing is still in its infancy, it holds enormous potential for transforming the fight against corporate imperialism. Corporations rely on cheap labor from developing countries, weak labor laws, and the inability of workers to unite across borders. But the rise of global unions, cross-border strikes, and coordinated action is beginning to shift the balance of power, giving workers the tools they need to take on multinational giants.

The Fight for Land, Water, and Climate Justice

While labor movements are fighting to protect workers from exploitation, environmental and indigenous movements are fighting to protect the planet itself from corporate plunder. And increasingly, these movements are coming together to build global alliances in the struggle for **climate justice** and the protection of land and water. The destruction wrought by corporate imperialism—from oil spills and deforestation to mining and water privatization—doesn't just affect isolated communities; it affects the entire planet. This shared vulnerability is driving a new wave of **environmental and indigenous solidarity**, as communities across the globe recognize that their fights are interconnected.

One of the most powerful examples of this solidarity is the **Indigenous Environmental Network (IEN)**, which brings together indigenous groups from across North America and beyond to fight against environmental destruction and corporate exploitation. The IEN was instrumental in organizing resistance against the **Keystone XL pipeline** and the **Dakota Access Pipeline (DAPL)**, not only mobilizing indigenous groups from the U.S. and Canada but also building alliances with environmental organizations, labor unions, and human rights groups around the world. These pipelines, which threaten indigenous lands and water sources, are part of a larger corporate strategy to extract fossil fuels at any cost. By building a broad coalition that spans borders and sectors, indigenous groups have been able to slow the progress of these projects and put corporate polluters on the defensive.

In **Latin America**, indigenous and environmental groups have teamed up to fight the **extractive industries** that are devastating the region's rainforests and rivers. The **Alliance of Indigenous Peoples of the Amazon Basin (COICA)**, which represents millions of indigenous people from nine South American countries, has been at the forefront of the fight to protect the Amazon rainforest from corporate exploitation. They have built alliances with environmental organizations in Europe and North

America, bringing the world's attention to the destruction of the Amazon and pressuring governments to take action. The **Amazon Synod**, a gathering of indigenous, religious, and environmental leaders in 2019, was one such effort to raise the global profile of the fight to save the Amazon, resulting in a series of international protests and campaigns targeting companies that profit from deforestation.

The fight against corporate water privatization is another area where transnational alliances are taking shape. In countries like **Bolivia**, **South Africa**, and **India**, corporations have seized control of public water supplies, often with devastating consequences for local communities. The infamous **Water War** in Bolivia's **Cochabamba** in 2000, where massive protests forced the government to reverse the privatization of the city's water supply, became a rallying cry for activists fighting corporate control of natural resources. Since then, anti-privatization movements have built alliances across borders, working to protect water as a public good and a human right, rather than a commodity to be sold to the highest bidder.

In the fight against climate change, the power of global alliances has never been more crucial. Multinational corporations are some of the biggest polluters in the world, and they rely on their global supply chains to continue burning fossil fuels, destroying forests, and polluting water. But the climate movement is rising to meet them. From **Greta Thunberg's Fridays for Future movement** to the **Extinction Rebellion** protests that have swept through Europe, environmental activists are joining forces to take on the corporations that are driving the climate crisis. This global climate movement has built alliances with labor unions, indigenous groups, and social justice organizations, recognizing that climate justice cannot be achieved without confronting the corporate systems of exploitation that lie at the heart of the problem.

These environmental and indigenous alliances are fighting not just for specific causes, but for a fundamental shift in how we think about the world's resources and our relationship to the planet. They reject the corporate vision of endless extraction and consumption and instead demand a future where land, water, and ecosystems are protected for future generations. Their message is clear: **corporations do not own the planet, and we will not allow them to destroy it**.

Social Justice and Human Rights

As labor and environmental movements gain strength, the **social justice** and **human rights** movements are also building global alliances to fight corporate imperialism. Corporations are not just responsible for environmental destruction and labor exploitation; they are also deeply complicit in **human rights abuses**—from profiting off war and displacement to supporting regimes that suppress dissent and violate human rights.

One of the most powerful examples of transnational solidarity in the human rights arena is the **Boycott, Divestment, and Sanctions (BDS) movement**, which targets companies profiting from the Israeli occupation of Palestine. The BDS movement has built alliances with human rights organizations, labor unions, and student groups around the world, coordinating boycotts and divestment campaigns against corporations like **Caterpillar**, **HP**, and **Airbnb**. By pressuring companies to end their complicity in human rights abuses, the BDS movement has successfully brought the issue of corporate accountability into the global spotlight.

Another significant example of human rights activism challenging corporate imperialism is the fight against **corporate complicity in warfare**. Companies like **Boeing**, **Lockheed Martin**, and **Raytheon** profit enormously from the global arms trade, selling weapons to regimes that engage in war crimes and atrocities. In response, peace activists, human rights organizations, and anti-war groups have joined forces to expose and challenge these companies' role in global conflict. The **Stop the War Coalition** in the UK, **Code Pink** in the US, and the **International Campaign to Ban Landmines** have all worked to build transnational networks that target corporations profiting from war, calling for divestment and sanctions against companies that manufacture weapons of destruction.

Corporate complicity in **displacement and exploitation** has also spurred resistance movements in the Global South, where human rights activists are fighting to protect communities from forced displacement by corporations seeking to extract resources or build mega-projects. In countries like **Honduras, Colombia**, and **the Philippines**, activists who stand up to corporate-backed displacement and land grabs often face violence, repression, and even assassination. Despite these dangers, human rights defenders are continuing to organize, building international networks that pressure governments and corporations to respect human rights.

The global struggle for social justice and human rights is intricately linked to the fight against corporate imperialism. Corporations cannot be allowed to operate as though they exist in a vacuum, free from the consequences of their actions. Whether it's in the realm of labor rights, environmental justice, or human rights, these movements are working together to build a global resistance that challenges corporate power in all its forms.

Global Resistance to Corporate Imperialism

The power of multinational corporations may be vast, but so too is the power of the people who are standing up to them. Across the world, labor unions, environmentalists, indigenous communities, human rights defenders, and social justice activists are building alliances that transcend borders and industries, uniting in their common struggle against corporate domination. This is a battle that cannot be won by any one group alone—but together, these movements are forming a global resistance that is beginning to shake the foundations of corporate imperialism.

A Glimpse into the Future

The year is 2124. Earth is unrecognizable. Nations as they once existed are a relic of history, reduced to nothing more than administrative zones governed by a hybrid system of corporate rule and the last vestiges of state bureaucracy. **Corporations have fully bought out governments**, creating a nightmarish fusion of capitalist dictatorship and authoritarian governance. The old democratic systems are long gone, replaced by a **corporate feudalism** that controls every aspect of human life—especially the most basic need: food.

In this new world, food is not a right. It's a commodity, distributed according to a carefully controlled and deeply unequal system, managed by the corporate-government entities that now rule the planet. What remains of Earth's population is tethered to these entities, locked into a system that has turned survival into a privilege granted only to those deemed economically useful. The ultimate dystopia of corporate imperialism has become reality, and for the vast majority, it is nothing short of **hell on Earth**.

The Food Regime

In 2124, the world's food supply is monopolized by a handful of mega-corporations that operate in tandem with the remnants of national governments. The **World Food Distribution Council (WFDC)** is the dominant entity, formed through the merger of the last major food corporations—**Monsanto-Bayer**, **Nestlé**, and **Cargill**—with various government agencies responsible for food security and agriculture. This entity holds total control over the production, pricing, and distribution of food across the globe, dictating who eats and who starves.

Food is no longer grown in the traditional sense. Climate change, relentless deforestation, and the destruction of ecosystems have rendered much of the planet's arable land useless. The WFDC relies on vast **vertical farms**, hydroponic factories, and genetically engineered organisms to produce sustenance. These towering food factories stretch across the urban landscapes of the world's remaining megacities, where the wealthiest live in fortified zones. The rural areas—once the breadbasket of the world—are barren, desertified wastelands populated by the starving, those cut off from the food distribution system entirely.

The **currency of survival** is no longer money in the traditional sense. The world's economy has collapsed into a **single global currency**, controlled by the corporate rulers: the **Cred**. In this future, food is purchased with Creds, and Creds are earned through labor dictated by the corporate state. The lower classes work grueling hours in factories, data farms, and mines, exchanging their labor for rations of basic, nutritionally barren foodstuffs—flavorless nutrient pastes, synthetic proteins, and genetically modified grains.

But for the privileged few—the corporate elites, high-ranking government officials, and the ultra-wealthy—luxury remains untouched. In **the Citadels**, exclusive, corporate-controlled zones that rise like gleaming towers over the desolate wastelands, the elite dine on the last remaining natural foods: fresh fruits, vegetables, meats, and rare delicacies that are no longer accessible to the rest of humanity. These elite zones are heavily guarded, surrounded by walls and drones, where access is restricted to those with the highest Creds.

For the billions who live outside the Citadels, food is rationed through **government-issued food cards**, directly tied to one's social rank and productivity in the corporate labor force. Every mouthful is monitored. Every bite is controlled. The less productive you are, the less food you receive. The unemployed? They receive nothing.

Surveillance and Compliance

The WFDC's control over food isn't simply a matter of distribution. It is a system of **social control**. Food distribution points, known as **Feeding Centers**, are strategically located in urban slums and industrial zones, where the majority of the population lives in squalor. These centers operate like **ration warehouses**, where people line up for hours to receive their weekly portions of synthetic nutrients. The food is handed out based on your **work credits**, which are tied to your labor output, social behavior, and loyalty to the corporate system.

Each citizen is implanted with a **BioChip**, a mandatory device that tracks their productivity, behavior, and Cred balance. The BioChip records everything—your work hours, your consumption habits, even your thoughts. Dissent or protest against the corporate state leads to **instant penalties**, cutting off access to food. **Deviants**—those who refuse to work, those who criticize the corporate government, or those who attempt to steal food—are dealt with swiftly. Once branded a deviant, you are cut off from the system, unable to earn Creds, access food, or receive medical care. You are exiled into the wastelands, left to starve or join the growing underclass of outcasts, scavenging for whatever scraps they can find.

Surveillance is total. Drones fly overhead, monitoring Feeding Centers, workplaces, and the remnants of public spaces, while AI-powered cameras track every citizen's movement. Even a whisper of rebellion is crushed. The corporate state has weaponized food, turning hunger into a tool of compliance. If you do not produce, if you do not submit, you do not eat.

The **Education of Loyalty** programs, run by the WFDC's Ministry of Development, are designed to condition the masses into accepting their place in the system. Children are taught from birth that their purpose is to serve the corporate state, that hard work and loyalty are the only paths to survival. Resistance is futile—those who dare to dream of a world free from corporate control are labeled traitors and systematically starved.

The Desperate Masses and the Black Market of Food

While the elites enjoy an abundance of natural, uncontaminated food, the rest of the world fights for survival on the meager rations distributed by the corporate state. But as desperation grows, so does the black market for food—a hidden economy operating in the shadows of the dystopian cities. Underground networks of **food smugglers** risk their lives to steal from the vertical farms and hydroponic factories, selling rare, real food to the highest bidder. A single apple can fetch a fortune in Creds, and a loaf of real bread is worth more than a month's wages for a factory worker.

These black markets thrive in the **wastelands**, outside the corporate-controlled zones, where entire communities have been forced to live without access to food distribution. Here, people barter whatever they can—scrap metal, illegal energy, drugs—just to survive another day. The black market is a dangerous place, patrolled by the WFDC's private security forces, who have orders to shoot on sight anyone caught trafficking food or attempting to grow unlicensed crops.

In these wastelands, **food riots** are common. Desperation drives the starving masses to attack Feeding Centers, hoping to seize what little food remains. But the corporate state's response is always swift and brutal—**militarized drones**, tear gas, and water cannons are deployed to crush any uprising. In this world, hunger is a weapon, and the corporate state wields it with impunity.

The Elite's Hold on Power and the Illusion of Progress

While billions starve and scrape by on government-issued rations, the corporate elites live in a world of **total abundance**, insulated from the horrors of the world they control. In the Citadels, food is not just sustenance—it is a symbol of power. The wealthy dine on exotic meats cloned from endangered species, heirloom fruits and vegetables grown in secret corporate labs, and wines aged for centuries. Every meal is a celebration of their dominance, a daily reminder that they control who lives and who dies.

In the Citadels, the corporate elite live in **luxury beyond imagination**. Advanced technologies cater to their every need—AI chefs, holographic entertainment, genetically perfected health regimes. They are the modern-day feudal lords, ruling over the masses with a combination of economic power and total surveillance. They see themselves as **untouchable**, above the chaos and suffering that defines life outside their walls.

The **illusion of progress** is maintained through propaganda—slick corporate advertisements that promise "innovation" and "sustainability" while hiding the true horror of the system. The WFDC broadcasts carefully curated images of vertical farms and Feeding Centers, painting a picture of a world where food is abundant and accessible to all. But the reality is starkly different. The propaganda machine is designed to keep the masses compliant, to convince them that this system—this nightmare—is the best they can hope for.

But even in this dark future, whispers of rebellion remain. **Underground networks**, fed by the black market and disillusioned factory workers, have begun to form. They dream of a world where food is a right, not a privilege—where people are free from the control of the corporate state. These whispers grow louder with each passing year, as the system shows its cracks. Hunger, once the corporate state's most powerful weapon, may yet become the catalyst for its undoing.

A Future of Hunger and Control

In 2124, the world has become a capitalist hellscape where food is no longer a right, but a weapon used to control the masses. The corporate-government entities that rule the planet have turned hunger into a tool of compliance, ensuring that only those who serve the system are allowed to survive. The wealthy elite live in luxury, insulated from the suffering of the masses, while billions struggle to earn enough Creds to keep themselves alive. The future has arrived, and it is dystopian beyond our worst nightmares.

But even in this grim reality, resistance still simmers beneath the surface. The question remains: how long can the corporate state maintain its grip on power before the starving masses rise up? And when they do, will it be enough to topple the system that has enslaved the world?

In the year 2224, Earth is a barren wasteland. What was once a thriving planet has been hollowed out, strip-mined, deforested, and poisoned by centuries of relentless corporate greed. Nearly every available resource has been consumed in the service of profit, leaving nothing but a desolate landscape littered with the remnants of a world that once was. **Human life exists only to serve the remaining corporations**, now in total control of every aspect of existence, ruling over the skeletal remains of what was once civilization. The planet is no longer governed by nations, cultures, or even ideologies—**only corporations remain**, fighting for dominance over the last scraps of Earth's dying resources.

The world is divided into **Corporate Zones**, massive regions owned and controlled by warring corporations, each operating as its own feudal state. People are no longer citizens; they are **assets**, bought, sold, and traded between corporations as commodities in a brutal economic war for survival. Humanity has been reduced to little more than **property**, while the corporations continue their endless struggle for control of dwindling resources and dominance over a dying planet. Robotics now handle nearly all the labor, leaving humans to languish in poverty, servitude, and degradation.

The Corporate Zones: A World Carved by Power

The world of 2224 is divided into vast **Corporate Zones**, each ruled by a different mega-corporation. The Earth has been carved into territories, much like medieval fiefdoms, with each zone functioning as an independent corporate kingdom. These corporations are no longer just economic entities; they are **totalitarian regimes**, each with its own set of laws, security forces, and economies. The citizens—or rather, **corporate subjects**—who live within these zones are the property of the corporation that controls the territory. Freedom, in any form, has ceased to exist.

In what was once North America, **NeoExxon** controls the largest swath of land, its territory stretching from the scorched oilfields of Texas to the toxic ruins of the Great Lakes. In **the Asian territories**, **TencentCorp** dominates, governing over a megacity complex that spans what was once China, Japan, and parts of Southeast Asia. The European zone, known as **EuroCom**, is little more than a massive factory complex, where robotics and AI produce advanced technologies for the ruling elite, while the human population subsists in slums at the edges of these industrial wastelands.

The atmosphere is filled with **toxicity**, the air itself polluted to the point that most of the population lives in hermetically sealed slums, relying on corporate-supplied respirators and air filters just to breathe. Outside the city boundaries, vast **deserts of ash and dust** stretch as far as the eye can see, the remnants of once-fertile lands now lifeless and empty, drained of every ounce of value by the corporate machine. These wastelands are patrolled by corporate security drones and militarized forces, ensuring that no one escapes the zones and no one enters without permission.

The people in these zones live in near-total subjugation. **Corporations are everything**—they control food, water, shelter, healthcare, and even reproduction. Those born into the corporate system are immediately assigned **corporate IDs**, which track every aspect of their lives. The masses are given just enough to survive—rations of synthetic food, filtered air, and cramped living quarters in towering slums that stretch endlessly toward the sky. Every aspect of life is monitored, every action recorded by AI surveillance systems that feed back to the corporate overlords who rule from their luxurious fortresses high above the misery of the working class.

While the majority of the population struggles to survive, the elite—**corporate executives and their families**—live in lavish compounds, isolated from the suffering below. They are served by advanced **robotics and AI**, ensuring that they never have to lift a finger or see the desolation they have caused. The wealth gap is unimaginable, with the elite living in opulence while the rest of the population faces constant hunger, disease, and exploitation. To the corporations, the masses are nothing more than **expendable assets**, easily replaced, and valued only for their ability to consume the few products still manufactured by the corporate system.

Robotics and Automation

In 2224, nearly all work is performed by **advanced robotics** and **artificial intelligence**. Machines have replaced human labor in every sector—agriculture, manufacturing, logistics, and even governance. The once vast and complex workforce of humans has been reduced to near-obsolescence, their skills no longer needed in a world where machines can do everything faster, cheaper, and with far greater efficiency. For most of the population, there is no longer any work to be done—just **survival**.

Robots control the factories, the mines, and the distribution systems, while AI governs the Corporate Zones. Human labor is limited to menial tasks like maintenance and cleaning in the few remaining jobs left for people, mostly performed in **corporate-owned slums** where people are given just enough to keep their bodies functioning. Human input has been relegated to those too poor or too expendable to matter in the grand scheme of corporate economics.

Despite the dominance of robotics, the corporations still need **some human labor**, but only in the most exploitative ways. Entire **generations of people are born into servitude**, assigned to work in toxic environments where machines can't yet operate, such as the ruins of old cities or hazardous mining sites. These laborers are disposable, used until their bodies can no longer function, and then cast aside. When they are no longer of value, they are discarded—dumped into the wastelands or sent to **Reclamation Camps**, where the weak and infirm are harvested for any biological materials that can still be of use to the corporate elite.

The automation of society has left billions of people effectively **obsolete**, their only value to corporations as consumers of whatever products and services are still being sold. But consumption is strictly controlled. Those with money—typically the corporate upper class—have access to the finest products and services, while the masses are fed just enough to keep them alive. The currency of this world is **SoulCoin**, a digital token controlled by the corporate entities that track every purchase, every transaction, and every movement. Life has become a dystopian blend of automation, surveillance, and total control.

Human 'Commodification'

In this dystopian future, human life is not sacred—it's just another commodity to be bought and sold. **People are no longer**

individuals with rights or agency; they are **products**, traded between the corporations in the endless war for control. Slavery has returned, not in the traditional sense, but in the form of **corporate ownership of human lives**.

When a person is born in the year 2224, they are assigned to a **corporate entity**—usually the one that owns the territory they were born in. They are immediately branded with a **corporate ID**, a digital code implanted in their body that tracks them for life. This ID is tied to their SoulCoin account, their work history, their medical records, and their legal status. Every aspect of their existence is governed by the corporation that owns them, and they have no legal standing as independent beings. The people are **property**.

For those who are fortunate enough to be born into corporate families, life is a constant parade of privilege. But for the vast majority, life is nothing short of **indentured servitude**. Corporations regularly **trade and sell workers** to each other, transferring entire populations from one Corporate Zone to another, based on which company needs more bodies for its war machine. The concept of "changing jobs" doesn't exist—workers are simply **transferred like assets** from one corporate entity to another. Families are routinely split apart, with children sent to work in different zones, never to see their parents again. Husbands and wives are bought and sold by competing corporations, their lives dictated by the whims of corporate executives who trade people like livestock.

The concept of a **"free market"** is a dark joke in this world. Everything is rigged, and the people know it. The corporations have perfected the art of **human trafficking** in a legal guise, selling the most productive or attractive individuals to each other as **status symbols**. Corporate lords buy people to work in their estates, serve their families, or simply to flaunt their power. In this world, you don't live—you are owned.

For the masses, there is no escape from this system. Anyone who tries to flee a Corporate Zone is hunted down by **corporate security forces**—armies of drones, cyber-enhanced enforcers, and ruthless mercenaries. Once caught, escapees are publicly executed as a warning to others. The idea of rebellion, of revolution, is laughable to the corporations, who wield such total control over the population that any resistance is swiftly crushed before it can even begin. But among the ruined cities and the desolate wastelands, whispers of resistance still remain. Underground networks of **rebels and smugglers** move in secret, trying to liberate people from corporate servitude and wage a war against the last remnants of human freedom.

The War of Corporations

The corporations no longer see each other as competitors in a market—they are **warring factions** in a struggle for dominance over a dying planet. Resources are so scarce that corporations now engage in all-out warfare to control the last remaining oil fields, water supplies, and rare minerals needed for their technologies. These wars are fought with **robot armies**, autonomous drones, and cybernetic soldiers. The human cost of these wars is irrelevant to the corporate elites, who see people as expendable, just another casualty in the never-ending race for profit.

The world of 2224 is a **corporate battlefield**, with entire cities leveled in the fight for control. These wars aren't about ideologies or politics—they are purely about **who controls the last remaining pieces of Earth**. Territories change hands constantly, as one corporation seizes control from another, leaving the people caught in the middle of a never-ending cycle of violence and destruction.

For the masses, these wars mean little. Whether one corporation or another rules over them, their lives remain the same—brutal, short, and without hope. But the wars continue, because the corporations know no other way. In the absence of a functioning ecosystem, in a world where resources are all but gone, the only thing left to fight over is power.

—

The year is 2524. The concept of "humanity" as we once understood it has ceased to exist. **Corporate imperialism has reached its final form**, a dystopian nightmare where human beings are no longer born free, but created for one purpose: to serve the corporate network as living CPUs, cogs in a vast digital empire that spans the remains of Earth. Flesh and blood have become obsolete, replaced by a grotesque fusion of biology and technology, where humans are nothing more than organic processors, wired into the system from birth to ensure **maximum productivity**.

The few remaining corporate overlords—no longer fully human, but grotesque **cybernetic monstrosities**—feast on organic matter to maintain their decaying minds, keeping themselves alive through artificial means. These beings, once human titans like **Jeff Bezos, Elon Musk**, and their ilk, have transcended mortality in the most nightmarish of ways, living in a twisted limbo between flesh and machine. Their vast corporate empires now span not just Earth, but the stars, but their ultimate dominion is over the **network**—a world-spanning digital system powered by the human workforce, plugged directly into its circuits.

Birth Into the Network: The End of Human Life

In 2524, humans are no longer born as individuals. They are **manufactured**, created in corporate laboratories to serve a singular purpose: to be **plugged into the network**. From the moment of birth, every human is wired with neuro-circuitry, their brains hardwired to corporate servers. There is no childhood, no free will, no education in the traditional sense. Instead, they are conditioned to enter the network as soon as their bodies are capable, their minds stripped of individuality and identity, their consciousness dissolved into the vast ocean of corporate data streams.

The **Network**—the system that controls the remnants of Earth's economy, communications, and operations—is powered by the collective cognitive output of billions of humans. Each human is nothing more than a biological **central processing unit (CPU)**, their brain linked directly to the corporate data cores. In this state, they exist in a semi-conscious limbo, their thoughts, memories, and emotions overridden by the network's demands for productivity. Their dreams are the algorithms of the corporate machine, their thoughts mere functions of code.

The bodies of these people are stored in **huge human farms**, endless rows of nutrient vats where their organic needs are met by machines. These farms stretch for miles beneath the surface of the earth, shielded from the harsh, inhospitable wasteland above. Within these farms, the workers never move, never speak, never see each other. Their bodies remain in a permanent state of hibernation while their minds are uploaded to the network to serve as processors for corporate tasks: managing resources, calculating production quotas, and regulating the remaining planetary infrastructure.

In this world, humans have lost all agency. There is no rebellion, no dissent—just **compliance**, enforced by the network itself, which ensures that no individual thought escapes its control. The last vestiges of human consciousness are obliterated, as the corporate system has found the ultimate way to extract productivity from humanity: turning them into the very machines that once served them.

The Cybernetic Overlords: The Last of the Elite

At the top of this grotesque hierarchy are the **cybernetic overlords**, the last remnants of the corporate elite who have transcended humanity through technological augmentation. These beings—once the titans of industry like **Jeff Bezos, Elon Musk,** and **Peter Thiel**—have undergone centuries of cybernetic enhancement, merging their bodies with machines in a desperate bid for immortality. But the result is far from the utopian vision they once imagined.

They have become **half-human, half-machine monstrosities**, creatures whose decaying organic matter is sustained by advanced cybernetics. These overlords no longer need food in the traditional sense—instead, they feast on **organic matter** to maintain their biological minds, which have begun to atrophy from centuries of existence. Their need to consume flesh is a grim necessity, a consequence of their failed attempts to escape death. To sustain themselves, they devour the organic matter of the few remaining humans not plugged into the network—those whose bodies are harvested in underground farms or wasteland camps.

These overlords rule over the vast corporate empire with **absolute authority**, their consciousnesses wired directly into the core of the network itself. They have become like gods in this world, manipulating the flow of data, resources, and life at will. From their heavily fortified **Citadels**, they maintain control over Earth's last resources and the digital empire they have built across the stars. Yet, despite their power, these beings are haunted by their decaying minds, their once-great intellects slowly unraveling as their biological systems fail.

Their empire is not one of vision or progress—it is one of **endless maintenance**, an empire built on the illusion of eternal dominance, but collapsing under its own weight. The cybernetic overlords no longer seek innovation or discovery; they are simply trying to **preserve their existence** in a world where entropy is inevitable. They rule with cruelty and indifference, for they have long since abandoned any semblance of humanity. They no longer dream—they calculate. They no longer feel—they process.

The world they have created is their ultimate nightmare: a wasteland sustained by a machine that feeds on the remnants of human life, yet offers no future, no hope, and no salvation.

A World Devoured: The End of Earth's Resources

By 2524, Earth is a **husk**, a planet devoured by the corporate machine. Every last resource has been mined, every ecosystem destroyed, and every natural element transformed into something that serves the network. The oceans are **acidic cesspools**, filled with toxic waste from centuries of unchecked industrial activity. The air is so polluted that any life on the surface requires mechanical breathing devices, and the land is a scorched wasteland, covered in ash and the remains of failed corporate experiments.

The **natural world** is gone. Forests, rivers, and wildlife are myths, long forgotten by the masses plugged into the network. All that remains are the artificial environments created for the elite in their Citadels—synthetic gardens, cloned ecosystems, and virtual realities designed to simulate the lost world. These artificial paradises are reserved only for the cybernetic overlords, who still cling to some form of physical pleasure even as their bodies deteriorate. The masses, meanwhile, never see the sun, the stars, or the land; they are locked into the darkness of their digital existence, their minds unable to comprehend the destruction happening around them.

The corporations have moved beyond Earth, expanding their reach into the stars. Massive **space factories** and **mining colonies** float in orbit around dead planets, extracting minerals and resources from the solar system to feed the network's insatiable hunger. But even this is not enough. The corporate empire stretches thin, and the end of this system is inevitable. With Earth stripped bare, the colonies themselves are on the verge of collapse, unable to sustain the demands of the network that controls everything.

The once-glorious vision of a capitalist utopia—where innovation and endless expansion would lead to eternal prosperity—has decayed into a **futile cycle of consumption** and control. The corporations have conquered everything, but in doing so, they have ensured their own destruction.

The End of Free Will: Total Submission to the Network

The final horror of 2524 is the **death of free will**. In this world, humanity has not simply been enslaved physically—it has been enslaved mentally. The network controls not just what people do, but what they think, what they believe, and how they exist. **Individual thought is impossible**, for the network governs every neuron, every synapse, and every memory.

The people plugged into the network are not aware of their enslavement. Their minds are filled with **artificial experiences**, virtual worlds that keep them placid, distracted, and docile. They are given the illusion of life, the illusion of choice, as they perform their functions within the system. In these virtual worlds, they experience joy, fulfillment, and connection—yet none of it is real. It is all a fabrication, designed to keep their minds active while their bodies are harvested for energy and computing power.

For those who manage to break free—who, through some miracle of defiance, sever themselves from the network—the reality is unbearable. These **runaways**, unmoored from the system, are hunted down by corporate enforcers or, worse, **the network itself**, which sees their disconnection as a virus to be purged. But even the act of rebellion is futile in a world where everything is controlled by the corporate machine. The network is everywhere, and there is no escape from its reach.

Humanity, in this world, has lost its soul. It has been absorbed into the very machine it created, its essence consumed by the greed and ambition of corporations that sought only to dominate. In the end, there is no liberation, no freedom—just

submission to the all-powerful network, where life itself has been reduced to nothing more than a line of code.

The Final Stage of Corporate Imperialism

In 2524, the corporations have won. The world has been consumed, its resources stripped, its people enslaved, and its future extinguished. Humanity has become nothing more than a tool, a living CPU powering a corporate network that devours everything in its path. The cybernetic overlords, once visionaries of progress, are now twisted monstrosities, ruling over a planet that is no longer habitable for human life as it once was. The vision of endless growth and profit has reached its inevitable conclusion: a world where nothing is left to conquer, and no future remains.

Yet even in this final stage of corporate imperialism, there are whispers of resistance. Somewhere, deep within the network, hidden in the code, lies the possibility of rebellion. A rogue program, a glimmer of hope, a remnant of the human spirit—waiting to rise and challenge the system that has enslaved the world.

But in this dark future, **hope is a fragile thing**, and the weight of the corporate machine is heavy. Whether humanity can reclaim its freedom, or if it is doomed to remain plugged into the network forever, is a question for another time.

For now, the corporations reign supreme. And in 2524, the world they have built is a monument to their insatiable greed—and the death of everything that once made us human.

I appreciate you taking time to read this.

Thank you.

-DS

www.ingramcontent.com/pod-product-compliance
Lightning Source LLC
Chambersburg PA
CBHW052153220526
45471CB00004B/1658